Passover from the Inside

A Jewish Guide for Christian Readers

Shira Schechter

Israel365

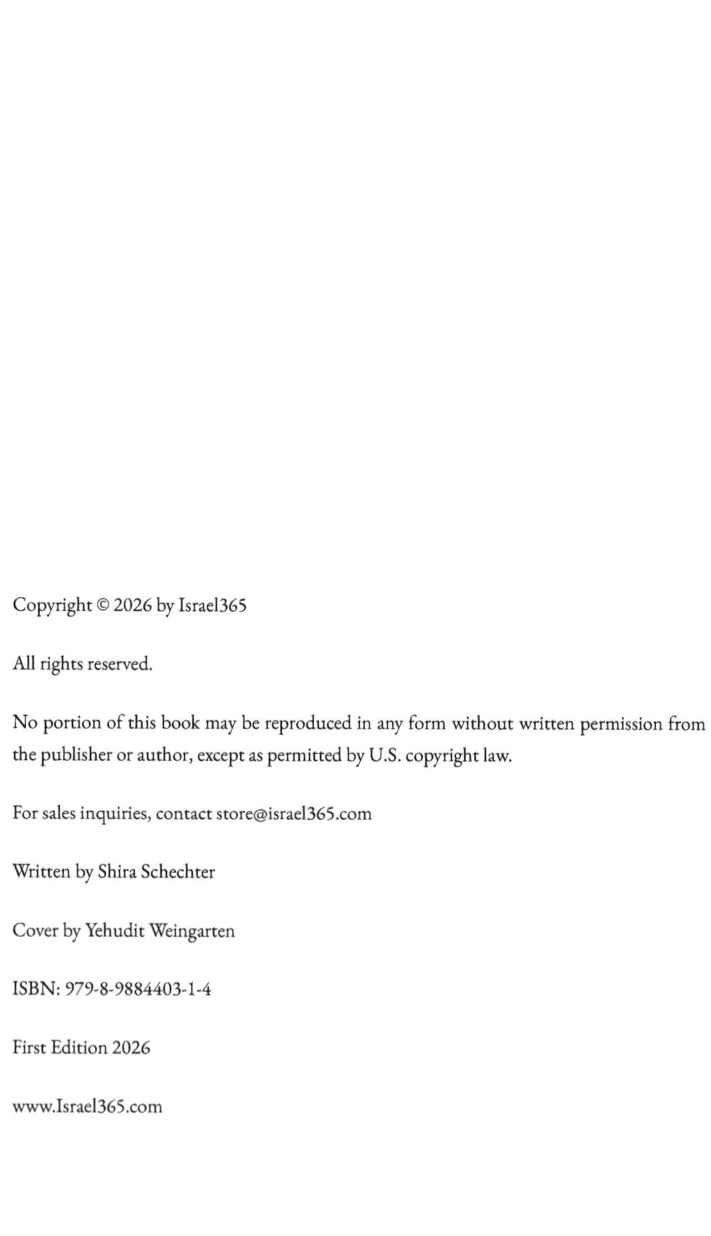

For sales inquiries, contact store@israel365.com

Written by Shira Schechter

Cover by Yehudit Weingarten

ISBN: 979-8-9884403-1-4

First Edition 2026

www.Israel365.com

Contents

Introduction: Join Us at the Passover Table

If you love Israel and the Jewish people, there's something essential you should know: you can't understand us from the outside. Jews have an unbroken tradition of reading, living, and passing down the Bible in ways that might be unfamiliar to many Christians. Without understanding how we read the Bible, shaped by our experience and interpreted by our sages, you can't genuinely know us. And right now, when Israel is under attack and the meaning of God's covenant with the Jewish people is being questioned even within the Christian world, genuine knowledge isn't optional. It's urgent.

Let's start with the text itself. The Torah wasn't written in English. The original Hebrew text is layered in ways that translation struggles to capture. Words connect to other words through sound and structure. Names reveal a person's character and destiny. The language itself carries layers of meaning that disappear when you translate. Translation captures the surface but loses the depth.

And the written text itself is only half the story. Jews don't read the Bible in isolation. We read it with the Sages' debates about what happened and why. We read it with Rashi's commentary sitting right alongside the verses. We read it with two thousand years of Jewish thought, prayer, and lived experience. This is the Oral Torah — the traditional interpretation handed down alongside the written text, given to Moses at Sinai together with the written words. The Jewish people who received the Torah didn't just get a book and figure it out for themselves. They got the book and the interpretation together. Two parts of one revelation.

And here is what that means for you as a Christian reader. The Bible you have read your entire life is, at its core, a Jewish book — written by Jews, lived by Jews, carried through history by Jews. Passover is not the background to that story. It is the story's beating heart. God chose a people. He looked at a world of nations and chose one and made them His own. Everything else in the Bible flows from that night. If you want to understand your scripture, you need to understand Passover the way we do.

This book brings you inside that tradition.

Every year, we gather at the Seder table to tell this story. Pull up a chair at our table, open our book, and hear the story that made us who we are — told in our words, understood through our tradition, still alive in our homes every single spring.

I believe this will enrich your faith, not threaten it. You'll see God's faithfulness in sharper focus. You'll read your Bible with new eyes. You'll understand the people you pray for not just as a political cause or a prophetic puzzle, but as we know ourselves.

Welcome to Passover.

Let me tell you about the night we left Egypt.

1

The Story of Passover

Every spring, Jewish families around the world sit down to an unusual meal. The table is set with strange foods: bitter herbs, a roasted bone, salt water, and a paste made from apples and nuts. Children ask rehearsed questions. Parents respond by telling a story that begins not with "once upon a time" but with an unusual declaration: "We were slaves to Pharaoh in Egypt, and the Lord our God brought us out from there."

Not *they* were slaves. *We* were slaves.

This is Passover, and it defies the normal rules of memory. Most historical commemorations look backward as we remember what happened to people in the past. But Passover demands something more radical: that we relive it. The *Haggadah*, the liturgical text that guides the *Seder* meal on the first night of the festival, explicitly commands: "In every generation, each person must see himself as though he personally went out from Egypt."

But why? Why must this ancient story of slavery and liberation be reenacted, retold, and relived every single year?

The Exodus was never just about escaping slavery. It was the birth of a nation—the moment God revealed His character to the world and bound Himself to Israel through covenant. This is why Jews don't just remember it; we relive it.

From the promise to Abraham through Moses' dramatic confrontation with Pharaoh, from the splitting sea to the fire at Sinai, this is the story of how a family became a people and how slaves became servants of God.

This is the story of Passover.

How Did the Israelites End Up in Egypt?

Long before the plagues struck the Egyptians, before Moses stood before Pharaoh, even before the first Hebrew brick was laid in Egypt, the story of Passover was already set in motion. The journey to Egypt began with a promise; a covenant between God and Abraham that would shape the destiny of his descendants for generations to come.

In a pivotal moment known as the Covenant Between the Parts, recorded in Genesis 15, Abraham received a troubling vision of the future. God instructed him to bring several animals, cut them in half, and arrange the pieces opposite each other. As the sun was setting, a deep sleep fell upon Abraham, and God revealed what lay ahead:

"Know well that your offspring shall be strangers in a land not theirs, and they shall be enslaved and oppressed four hundred years; but I will execute judgment on the nation they shall serve, and in the end they shall go free with great wealth. As for you, You shall go to your fathers in peace; You shall be buried at a ripe old age. And they shall return here in the fourth generation, for the iniquity of the Amorites is not yet complete." (Genesis 15:13-16)

This prophecy laid out the entire arc before it began—enslavement, suffering, redemption, and return. Two promises intertwined: Abraham's children would be enslaved and eventually freed, and they would inherit the Land of Israel. But how would this prophecy unfold?

Joseph: The Path to Egypt

The actual descent to Egypt came through a family drama that would shape Israel's history. Joseph, Abraham's great-grandson and Jacob's favored son, sparked his brothers' jealousy:

"And when his brothers saw that their father loved him more than any of his brothers, they hated him so that they could not speak a friendly word to him." (Genesis 37:4)

That hatred nearly cost Joseph his life. Instead, it cost him his freedom:

"When Midianite traders passed by, they pulled Joseph up out of the pit. They sold Joseph for twenty pieces of silver to the Ishmaelites, who brought Joseph to Egypt." (Genesis 37:28)

But what seemed like tragedy was actually divine providence. Through a remarkable series of events—slavery, false imprisonment, and finally, the interpretation of Pharaoh's dreams—Joseph rose to become viceroy of Egypt, second only to Pharaoh himself.

Through Pharaoh's dream, Joseph understood that seven years of abundance would be followed by seven years of devastating famine.

After Pharaoh made him viceroy of Egypt, Joseph acted decisively: "So he collected all the grain of the seven years that the land of Egypt was enjoying, and stored the grain in the cities; he put in each city the grain of the fields around it... So Joseph collected produce in very large quantity, like the sands of the sea, until he ceased to measure it, for it could not be measured." (Genesis 41:48-49)

Joseph collected more than enough grain to support the Egyptian people. When famine struck, it reached beyond Egypt to Canaan, where Jacob and his remaining sons struggled to survive. Hearing that grain was available in Egypt, Jacob sent his sons to buy food. They had no idea they would be standing before the brother they had sold into slavery years earlier.

After a complex series of encounters that included tests and accusations, Joseph could no longer contain himself: "Joseph said to his brothers, 'I am Joseph. Is my father still well?' But his brothers could not answer him, so dumfounded were they on account of him" (Genesis 45:3).

Imagine that moment. The powerful Egyptian official they had been negotiating with was their own brother; the one they had betrayed, the one they thought was lost forever. Joseph, weeping, assured them of his forgiveness and urged them to bring their entire family to Egypt:

"You will dwell in the region of Goshen, where you will be near me—you, your children, and your grandchildren, your flocks and herds, and all that is yours. There I will provide for you—for there are yet five years of famine to come—that you and your household and all that is yours may not suffer want." (Genesis 45:10-11)

Jacob's Fear and God's Promise

But Jacob did not rush eagerly to Egypt. He went with deep trepidation.

Why? Jacob remembered the prophecy given to his grandfather Abraham, that his descendants would be strangers in a foreign land, enduring servitude for generations. The 13th-century French commentator Rabbi Hezekiah ben Manoah (known as the Chizkuni) explains that Jacob understood this journey might mark the beginning of that dark prophecy.[1]

God appeared to Jacob in a vision, addressing his fears directly:

"God called to Israel in a vision by night: 'Jacob! Jacob!' He answered, 'Here.' And He said, 'I am God, the God of your father. Fear not to go down to Egypt, for I will make you there into a great nation. I Myself will go down with you to Egypt, and I Myself will also bring you back; and Joseph's hand shall close your eyes.'" (Genesis 46:2-4)

The message was clear: Yes, the exile foretold to Abraham was beginning. But so too was the promise that Jacob's family would grow into a great nation. And most importantly, God would not abandon them there. He Himself would bring them back to their land.

Jacob's entire family descended to Egypt. They settled in Goshen, a fertile region where they could maintain their distinct identity and practices (Genesis 47:27).

---

1. Chizkuni, Genesis 46:3

The Israelites went to Egypt to survive a famine, but they stayed. Over time, their population grew large enough to attract the attention of the state. Pharaoh responded by enslaving them, turning a resident minority into a labor force just as God had told Abraham would happen.

But why did God orchestrate such a painful journey for His chosen people? Why did Israel have to experience hundreds of years of slavery before receiving the Torah and returning to the Holy Land?

Rabbi Yaakov Tzvi Mecklenburg (1785–1865) explains that Egyptian slavery functioned as a refining crucible. In fact, the Bible itself calls Egypt exactly that: an iron crucible (Deuteronomy 4:20). God's purpose was to purify the Israelites of their baser characteristics, burning away the dross so that only pure gold would remain. Many of those who were unworthy died during the plague of darkness,[2] and only those who remained were chosen to receive the Torah. By the time the Israelites left Egypt, they were no longer just a family that shared ancestry — they were a people refined by fire, ready to stand at Sinai and receive God's law.[3]

From the beginning, God made clear that being His chosen nation would not be an easy path. Israel's story does not begin with comfort but with centuries of slavery, because character is not formed in ease. Endurance, responsibility, and moral seriousness are learned under pressure, not in safety. Egypt was not a detour from Israel's mission; it

---

2. Rashi, Exodus 10:22

3. Rabbi Yaakov Tzvi Mecklenburg, *Haketav Vehakabbalah*, Deuteronomy 4:20

was the first stage of it. The hardship was necessary to shape a people capable of carrying God's law, sustaining it, and surviving history with it intact.

The Oppression Begins

The Book of Exodus begins with remarkable growth: "But the Israelites were fertile and prolific; they multiplied and increased very greatly, so that the land was filled with them" (Exodus 1:7).

The descendants of Jacob thrived in Egypt, fulfilling God's ancient promise to Abraham. But their success was short-lived.

A new Pharaoh arose, one who had no memory of Joseph and no gratitude for how this Hebrew family had saved Egypt from famine. All he saw was a threat:

"A new king arose over Egypt who did not know Joseph. And he said to his people, 'Look, the Israelite people are much too numerous for us. Let us deal shrewdly with them, so that they may not increase; otherwise in the event of war they may join our enemies in fighting against us and rise from the ground.'" (Exodus 1:8-10)

Fear breeds cruelty. Pharaoh's solution was systematic oppression. First came the forced labor (Exodus 1:11). But oppression backfired. The more the Egyptians afflicted the Israelites, the more they multiplied (Exodus 1:12).

So Pharaoh escalated: "And they made their lives bitter with hard labor at mortar and bricks and with all sorts of tasks in the field" (Exodus 1:14).

The Israelites continued to grow despite Pharaoh's efforts to control them. When backbreaking labor failed to slow their expansion, he turned to an extreme measure: the murder of Israelite newborn males. Rashi explains that Pharaoh's astrologers had foreseen the rise of a male deliverer, so he moved to eliminate the threat at its source.[4]

Fortunately for the Israelites, their heroic midwives refused to comply: "The midwives, fearing God, did not do as the king of Egypt had told them; they let the boys live" (Exodus 1:17).

According to the sages, these heroic women, Shiphrah and Puah, were none other than Jochebed and Miriam, who would later become Moses' mother and sister. They risked their lives to preserve the next generation.

Enraged by their defiance, Pharaoh issued a brutal public decree: every Hebrew male child must be cast into the Nile River (Exodus 1:22). Into this world of terror and violence, Moses was born.

A Child Hidden, A Leader Forged

Moses' mother hid him for three months. When she could no longer conceal him, she made a desperate choice—she placed him in a waterproofed basket among the reeds of the Nile, the very river meant to be his grave.

There, Pharaoh's daughter discovered him:

---

4. Rashi, Exodus 1:16

"The daughter of Pharaoh came down to bathe in the Nile, while her maidens walked along the Nile. She spied the basket among the reeds and sent her slave girl to fetch it. When she opened it, she saw that it was a child, a boy crying. She took pity on it and said, 'This must be a Hebrew child.'" (Exodus 2:5-6)

In a moment of compassion that defied her father's decree, she chose to save the child. Moses' sister Miriam, who had been watching from a distance, quickly arranged for the baby's own mother to nurse him. Divine Providence had intervened: Moses would grow up in Pharaoh's palace while maintaining a connection to his Hebrew roots—a dual identity that would prepare him for his life's mission.[5]

Years later, the young prince witnessed an Egyptian taskmaster savagely beating a Hebrew slave. Something stirred within him; a connection to his people, a sense of justice that royal privilege couldn't suppress. He killed the Egyptian and buried the body in the sand.

When Moses realized his deed was known, he fled to Midian, trading a prince's life for a shepherd's existence. He married, tended flocks, and might have lived out his days in quiet obscurity.

But God had other plans.

One ordinary day, while tending his father-in-law's flock, Moses witnessed something extraordinary: "An angel of the Lord appeared to him in a blazing fire out of a bush. He gazed, and there was a bush all aflame, yet the bush was not consumed" (Exodus 3:2).

When Moses turned aside to investigate this wonder, God called his name and revealed a mission that would change history:

"And the Lord continued, 'I have marked well the plight of My people in Egypt and have heeded their outcry because of their taskmasters; yes, I am mindful of their sufferings... Come, therefore, I will send you to Pharaoh, and you shall free My people, the Israelites, from Egypt.'" (Exodus 3:7, 10)

Moses balked. Five times, he questioned his fitness for the task. Who am I to go to Pharaoh? What if they don't believe me? I'm not eloquent. Please send someone else!

But God persisted, providing signs to validate Moses' mission and appointing his brother Aaron as his spokesman. Rabbi Samson Raphael Hirsch[6] notes the irony: Moses' very humility—his sense of inadequacy—was precisely what qualified him for leadership.

Reluctantly, Moses accepted his calling.

Moses Confronts Pharaoh

Moses and Aaron stood before the most powerful ruler in the ancient world and made an audacious demand:

"Thus says the Lord, the God of Israel: Let My people go that they may celebrate a festival for Me in the wilderness." (Exodus 5:1)

Pharaoh's response dripped with contempt:

---

6. Rabbi Samson Raphael Hirsch, Exodus 3:11

"Who is the Lord that I should heed Him and let Israel go? I do not know the Lord, nor will I let Israel go." (Exodus 5:2)

Not only did he refuse, he made things worse. From that day forward, the Israelites would have to gather their own straw while maintaining the same quota of bricks. The people's suffering intensified, and they turned on Moses in anger.

It seemed Moses' mission had failed before it truly began. But this was only the opening move in a cosmic confrontation between divine power and human arrogance.

What followed was a systematic dismantling of Egyptian power and pride through ten devastating plagues:

1. Water turned to blood
2. Frogs
3. Lice
4. Wild beasts
5. Pestilence
6. Boils
7. Hail
8. Locusts
9. Darkness
10. Death of the firstborn

But these plagues were more than punishments; they were lessons. The Bible emphasizes this repeatedly:

"And the Egyptians shall know that I am the Lord, when I stretch out My hand over Egypt and bring out the Israelites from their midst." (Exodus 7:5)

"Thus says the Lord, 'By this you shall know that I am the Lord.'" (Exodus 7:17)

"For this time I will send all My plagues upon your person, and your courtiers, and your people, in order that you may know that there is none like Me in all the world." (Exodus 9:14)

The plagues were meant to teach. Each one showed, step by step, that Egypt's gods, Pharaoh's authority, and the natural order itself were not truly in control. Pharaoh was being confronted, but so were the Israelites, who had lived under Egyptian power for generations and needed to see that it could be broken.

Rabbi Isaac Abarbanel offers a brilliant framework for understanding the plagues' structure. According to him, Pharaoh's arrogance rested on three denials:[7]

First, he denied God's very existence. "I do not know the Lord," he declared, attributing the world's governance to nature and celestial forces rather than a supreme Deity.

7. Abarbnel, Exodus 7:19

Second, he denied divine providence. Even if such a God existed, Pharaoh believed He had no authority over earthly rulers. "Who is the Lord that I should obey His voice?"

Third, he denied God's power to alter nature at will, which explained his stubborn refusal to heed Moses' warnings despite the miraculous signs.

Abarbanel explains that the plagues systematically dismantled these denials:

The first three plagues (blood, frogs, and lice) established God's existence. "By this you shall know that I am the Lord" (Exodus 7:17).

The next three plagues (wild beasts, pestilence, and boils) demonstrated divine providence, that God actively supervises human affairs and judges accordingly. "That you may know that I am the Lord *in the midst of the land*" (Exodus 8:18).

The final set (hail, locusts, and darkness) proved God's absolute power over nature. "So that you may know that there is none like Me in all the earth" (Exodus 9:14).

The tenth plague—the death of the firstborn—served as divine retribution for Pharaoh's own decree to drown Hebrew children in the Nile.

The Ten Plagues weren't just about punishment; they were an elaborate lesson in theology, teaching not just Pharaoh, but all of humanity and all future generations about the nature of divine power, providence, and presence in our world.

Yet after each plague, Pharaoh hardened his heart. Rabbi Obadiah Seforno clarifies what this "hardening" meant: not the removal of Pharaoh's free will, but rather the strengthening of his resolve. God gave him the fortitude to withstand punishments that would otherwise have forced a surrender based on self-preservation rather than genuine repentance. Pharaoh needed the capacity to choose freely—and he chose defiance.[8]

The tenth plague finally shattered Pharaoh's resistance. At midnight, death swept through Egypt, striking the firstborn in every household:

"And Pharaoh arose in the night, with all his courtiers and all the Egyptians—because there was a loud cry in Egypt; for there was no house where there was not someone dead. He summoned Moses and Aaron in the night and said, 'Up, depart from among my people, you and the Israelites with you! Go, worship the Lord as you said!'" (Exodus 12:30-31)

The proud king who had asked, "Who is the Lord?" now knew. The ruler who had enslaved God's people now begged them to leave. The confrontation was over; Pharaoh and Egypt were defeated.

The Exodus was about to begin.

Sanctifying Time

This dramatic moment was the culmination of careful preparation. In the days before that fateful night, God gave the Israelites detailed instructions for what they would need to do. And He began not with

---

8. Seforno, Exodus 7:3

the dramatic Passover sacrifice itself, but with something that might seem surprisingly mundane for such a momentous occasion:

"This month shall be to you the beginning of months; it shall be the first month of the year to you." (Exodus 12:2)

The Hebrew word for "this" indicates something visible and immediate. Rashi explains that God showed Moses the moon in its first stage of renewal, the thin crescent that marks a new lunar cycle, and said: "When the moon renews itself like *this*, that shall be the beginning of the month for you." God was teaching Moses how to recognize the new moon and, by extension, how to establish the Jewish calendar.[9]

This wasn't merely an astronomy lesson. God was transferring authority to the Jewish people to sanctify time itself. The court in Israel would determine, based on witnesses who testified to seeing the new moon, when each month officially began. And since all the festivals are dated to specific days of specific months—Passover on the fifteenth of *Nisan*, *Shavuot* fifty days later, and *Sukkot* on the fifteenth of the seventh month—the power to sanctify the new moon meant the power to determine when God's calendar would unfold.

Rabbi Obadiah Seforno captures the deeper significance of why they were given this command at this time. Until this moment, the Israelites had no control over their own time. Slaves don't set their own schedules. Every hour belonged to Pharaoh, and every day was measured by taskmasters' quotas. Now, on the eve of their freedom, God gave them sovereignty over time itself. They would decide when months begin, when festivals arrive, and how the year unfolds. Time would

9. Rashi, Exodus 12:2

no longer be imposed upon them by their masters—it would be theirs to sanctify. In essence, by giving them this command now, God was declaring their freedom.[10]

And this particular month, the month of spring and redemption, would become the beginning of all months, the first month in the sacred calendar. Not because of its agricultural significance or its position in the solar year, but because the Exodus happened then. As Rashi notes, this month would be the first in the counting, making *Iyar* the second month, *Sivan* the third, and so forth. Time itself would now be measured from this moment of liberation. Everything that came before was prologue; everything after would unfold in reference to this defining event.

Establishing the calendar was only the beginning of God's instructions. He also gave detailed commands about how they were to observe this first Passover—rituals that would both protect them on that fateful night and establish a festival for all generations.

The Exodus

The Israelites were to perform a ritual unlike anything they had done before (Exodus 12:3-11). On the tenth day of the Hebrew month of *Nisan*, each household was to select a lamb, keep it for four days, and then slaughter it in the afternoon of the fourteenth. They were to paint its blood on their doorposts and lintels, then roast the meat to eat with bitter herbs and unleavened bread:

---

10. Seforno, Exodus 12:2

"They shall take some of the blood and put it on the two doorposts and the lintel of the houses in which they are to eat it... And the blood on the houses where you are shall be a sign for you: when I see the blood I will pass over you, so that no plague will destroy you when I strike the land of Egypt." (Exodus 12:7, 13)

This first Passover sacrifice required extraordinary courage. The Egyptians worshiped sheep as sacred animals. By publicly slaughtering what their oppressors considered divine and marking their homes with its blood, the Israelites made a radical declaration: they rejected Egyptian idolatry and placed their faith entirely in God's protection.

The next morning, as the Egyptians mourned the death of their firstborn, the Israelites departed in such haste that their bread dough had no time to rise:

"And they baked unleavened cakes of the dough that they had taken out of Egypt, for it was not leavened, since they had been driven out of Egypt and could not delay; nor had they prepared any provisions for themselves." (Exodus 12:39)

This is one reason why we eat *matzah* (unleavened bread) during Passover. It's the taste of the bread of redemption baked in haste.

As the Israelites began their journey toward the Promised Land, God made His presence unmistakable: "The Lord went before them in a pillar of cloud by day, to guide them along the way, and in a pillar of fire by night, to give them light, that they might travel day and night" (Exodus 13:21).

But God didn't lead them by the most direct route to Canaan. That path would have taken them through Philistine territory, where war would have tempted them to retreat (Exodus 13:17). Instead, they headed toward the Red Sea—a route that would soon seem like a trap.

Pharaoh immediately regretted his decision to allow the Israelites to leave Egypt. The ruler who had begged them to leave now pursued them with his entire army: "The Egyptians gave chase to them, and all the chariot horses of Pharaoh, his horsemen, and his warriors overtook them encamped by the sea..." (Exodus 14:9).

The Israelites found themselves in an impossible situation with the sea before them and the Egyptian army behind them. Panic set in. Had they escaped slavery only to die in the wilderness?

But Moses stood firm:

"But Moses said to the people, 'Have no fear! Stand by, and witness the deliverance which the Lord will work for you today; for the Egyptians whom you see today you will never see again. The Lord will battle for you; you hold your peace!'" (Exodus 14:13-14)

Then God commanded Moses to lift his staff over the sea. All night, a strong east wind blew, pushing back the waters and creating a path of dry land: "The Israelites went into the sea on dry ground, the waters forming a wall for them on their right and on their left" (Exodus 14:22). Imagine walking between those towering walls of water, each step an act of faith.

The Egyptians, emboldened, pursued them into the sea. But as the last Israelite reached the opposite shore, Moses stretched out his hand again. The waters crashed down, drowning Pharaoh's entire army.

The splitting of the Red Sea was more than a miraculous rescue; it was a deep spiritual awakening. As the waters parted and then engulfed their oppressors, something fundamental shifted within the Israelites, strengthening their belief in God:

"And when Israel saw the wondrous power which the Lord had wielded against the Egyptians, the people feared the Lord; they had faith in the Lord and His servant Moses." (Exodus 14:31)

According to the sages, the revelation at the sea surpassed even the visions of the great prophets. Even the humblest maidservant witnessed divine glory more extraordinary than what Ezekiel would later see.[11]

In overwhelming gratitude, Moses and the Israelites burst into song (Exodus 15:1). This Song at the Sea is recited daily in Jewish prayers, keeping alive the memory of this moment when God's power was made manifest, and His sovereignty was proclaimed.

The Covenant at Sinai

From the shores of the Red Sea, the Israelites journeyed through the wilderness toward their ultimate destination: Mount Sinai, where they would receive the Torah and be transformed from freed slaves into a nation with a divine purpose.

Almost seven weeks after leaving Egypt, the Israelites arrived at Mount Sinai:

"On the third new moon after the Israelites had gone forth from the land of Egypt, on that very day, they entered the wilderness of Sinai." (Exodus 19:1)

---

11. Yalkut Shimoni, Beshalach, 247

At this desert mountain, God proposed a covenant:

"Now then, if you will obey Me faithfully and keep My covenant, you shall be My treasured possession among all the peoples. Indeed, all the earth is Mine, but you shall be to Me a kingdom of priests and a holy nation." (Exodus 19:5-6)

The people responded without hesitation:

"All the people answered as one, saying, 'All that the LORD has spoken we will do!'" (Exodus 19:8)

God then instructed Moses to prepare the people for something unprecedented—a direct divine revelation to an entire nation. The people sanctified themselves, washed their garments, and established a boundary around the mountain. On the third day, heaven and earth converged:

"Now Mount Sinai was all in smoke, for the Lord had come down upon it in fire; the smoke rose like the smoke of a kiln, and the whole mountain trembled violently." (Exodus 19:18)

Amid thunder, lightning, thick cloud, and the piercing sound of the *shofar* (ram's horn), God spoke the Ten Commandments directly to all the people, a unique event in human history:

1. I am the Lord your God who brought you out of the land of Egypt. (Exodus 20:2)

2. You shall have no other gods nor make any graven images. (Exodus 20:3-6)

3. You shall not take the name of the Lord in vain. (Exodus

20:7)

4. Remember the Sabbath day to keep it holy. (Exodus 20:8-11)
5. Honor your father and mother. (Exodus 20:12)
6. You shall not murder. (Exodus 20:13)
7. You shall not commit adultery. (Exodus 20:13)
8. You shall not steal. (Exodus 20:13)
9. You shall not bear false witness. (Exodus 20:13)
10. You shall not covet anything that belongs to your neighbor. (Exodus 20:14)

These ten commandments are not more important than the rest of the 613 commandments of the Torah. Rather, Rabbi Saadia Gaon (882–942 CE), the great Babylonian Jewish thinker, explains that they serve as foundational principles under which all the others can be organized. Each functions as a category heading, with the detailed laws revealed subsequently to Moses on the mountain fitting beneath these broader themes.[12]

Why Sinai Matters

The revelation at Sinai was significant for multiple reasons. Rabbi Judah Halevi (c. 1075–1141), the Sephardic poet and philosopher, argued in his work, *The Kuzari*, that this mass revelation to millions of witnesses distinguishes Judaism from all other faiths. Unlike claims

12. Cited in Rashi on Exodus 24:12

based on individual visions, this collective experience cannot be fabricated or distorted through transmission.

But there's something even deeper here. The medieval scholar Nachmanides (c. 1194-1270) explains that the Exodus was not completed at the Red Sea. Physical freedom was only the beginning: "When they came to Mount Sinai and made the Tabernacle, and the Holy One, blessed be He, caused His Divine Presence to dwell again amongst them, they returned to the status of their fathers when the counsel of God was upon their tents... Then they were considered redeemed."[13]

Liberation from slavery was merely the precondition for spiritual freedom through Torah. As God told Moses at the burning bush: "When you have freed the people from Egypt, you shall worship God at this mountain." (Exodus 3:12). The destination was always Sinai.

This is why the first of the Ten Commandments identifies God specifically as "the One who brought you out of the land of Egypt." The Jewish people's relationship with God rests not only on His role as Creator, which applies to all humanity, but on His role as Redeemer. The Exodus created a special relationship that was sealed through the covenant at Sinai.

Only by becoming servants of God did the Israelites achieve true freedom. Their role in the world was now clear: they would journey to the Promised Land and establish a society governed by divine law. In Israel, the Torah's full expression could be realized. This was the land promised to their forefathers — the same land God had pointed to when He told Abraham at the Covenant of the Parts that his

---

13. Nachmanides, Introduction to Exodus

descendants would one day return. This was where they could fulfill their mission of being "a light unto the nations." As Isaiah prophesied: "For instruction shall come forth from Zion, The word of the Lord from Jerusalem" (Isaiah 2:3).

When Joshua would lead them across the Jordan, both halves of that ancient promise would be complete: the exile endured, the redemption accomplished, and the people home.

An Eternal Commandment

The story of the Exodus didn't end with Joshua. Before the Israelites even left Egypt, God commanded that this narrative—from slavery to redemption to covenant—must be relived every year:

"This day shall be to you one of remembrance: you shall celebrate it as a festival to the Lord throughout the ages; you shall celebrate it as an institution for all time." (Exodus 12:14)

"And you shall observe this as an institution for all time, for you and for your descendants." (Exodus 12:24)

Every spring, Jewish families gather around tables set with the same symbols their ancestors ate in Egypt: bitter herbs recalling the bitterness of slavery, unleavened bread baked in haste, wine celebrating freedom. Children ask questions. Parents tell the story. Through the annual observance of Passover, that transformative journey from slavery to freedom to covenant remains alive, continually shaping Jewish identity and faith across the millennia.

And in doing so, we remember what God told Abraham at the Covenant of the Parts. The exile, the suffering, the redemption, the return — none of it was accident or tragedy that God later repaired. It was the plan, announced before it began, executed with precision across centuries. Every Passover *Seder* is a declaration that the God who made that promise kept it, and every retelling is an act of faith that He will keep the promises still outstanding.

From Story to Living Tradition

This is the story I promised to bring you inside. From God's promise to Abraham through slavery in Egypt, from the plagues and the splitting sea to the covenant at Sinai—you've now heard the full arc of the Exodus as Jews tell it.

But knowing the story is just the beginning. The Exodus stands at the center of biblical faith. The prophets invoke it constantly. The Psalms celebrate it. God Himself identifies as "the One who brought you out of Egypt" throughout Scripture. This isn't just ancient history; it's the defining event that shaped how the biblical world understood God, freedom, redemption, and covenant.

Yet there's a dimension to Passover that you can't access through reading the story alone. The Jewish people don't just study Passover—they live it. In the chapters ahead, we'll explore what Passover means and how it's practiced.

Collected Insights

What We're Missing About Passover

Shira Schechter

Passover is not, at its core, about freedom. That might sound strange coming from a holiday we literally call *zeman cheiruteinu* — the time of our liberation. But Rabbi Yehuda Henkin cuts through that assumption with a single sentence: "Pesach is the holiday of belief in God."

Not liberation. Belief.

Look at what the Torah actually says about why the plagues happened. God tells Moses explicitly: "I have hardened Pharaoh's heart in order that I may display these My signs among them — and that you may know that I am God" (Exodus 10:1-2). The plagues weren't just the mechanism of escape. They were a curriculum. God was teaching something.

The lesson sank in. After the sea split and the Egyptian army drowned, the Torah records: "The people feared the Lord; they had faith in the Lord and His servant Moses" (Exodus 14:31). Freedom and faith arrived together — but faith was the point.

This is why the Ten Commandments don't begin with creation. God doesn't say, "I am the Lord your God who made heaven and earth." He says, "I am the Lord your God who brought you out of the land of Egypt." The Exodus, not the creation, is the foundation of Jewish faith. God reveals Himself not through abstract theology but through action in history.

The *Haggadah* (the text that guides the Passover *Seder*) knows this. It insists that even scholars — people who know the story cold — are obligated to recount the Exodus at length, and the more you recount it the better. If this were just history, repetition would be redundant. But if the purpose is to strengthen belief by reliving the experience of divine intervention, then repetition isn't redundant. It's the whole point.

The *Haggadah* goes further. The section of *Vehi she'amdah* — "This promise has stood by our ancestors and ourselves" — extends the Exodus into every generation. "In every generation they rise up to destroy us, and the Holy One, blessed be He, delivers us from their hands." The Exodus isn't a founding event frozen in the past. It's a template for reading all of Jewish history.

We may be living in the early chapters of that template playing out again. The survival of the Jewish people through centuries of persecution, expulsion, and genocide, followed by the rebirth of Israel in its ancient homeland, is not a story that chance explains. No historian of ancient peoples would have predicted that the nation exiled from its land two thousand years ago would return, revive its language, and rebuild its state. And yet here we are.

After October 7th, when terrorists massacred over 1,200 people and took hundreds hostage, the words of the *Haggadah* landed differently. "In every generation they rise up against us" was no longer a historical observation — it was the morning news. Jews around the world who had recited those words perfunctorily for years suddenly heard them as if for the first time. The surge of global antisemitism that followed, the protests celebrating massacre, the institutions that looked away — all of it felt hauntingly familiar to anyone who knew Jewish history. We had been here before. Many times. And we were still here.

That is the faith Passover is trying to build. Not a naive faith that suffering won't come, but a resilient faith that knows how the story ends. When we raise the final cup at the *Seder* and say "Next year in Jerusalem," we're not expressing nostalgia. We're expressing conviction — that the God who took us out of Egypt is not finished with us yet.

Fire Not Water: God's Mysterious Command for the Passover Sacrifice

Rabbi Elie Mischel

In the months before October 7th, Israel looked like a nation coming apart. Hundreds of thousands of Israelis were in the streets protesting judicial reforms. Reservists were threatening to refuse service. Commentators across the political spectrum were asking openly whether Israeli democracy could survive. Yahya Sinwar, watching from Gaza, liked what he saw. A fractured nation, he calculated, was a vulnerable one. The moment was right.

He was catastrophically wrong.

The Bible offers us clear insight into why through God's instructions for the Passover sacrifice:

"They shall eat the flesh that same night; they shall eat it roasted over the fire, with unleavened bread and with bitter herbs. Do not eat any of it raw, or cooked in any way with water, but roasted—head, legs, and entrails—over the fire." (Exodus 12:8-9)

Why did God insist on roasting rather than boiling? The difference reveals everything about how God forms His people. When meat is boiled, it absorbs water, becoming softer until it eventually falls apart, with fibers separating and structure dissolving. But roasting does the opposite — fire draws out excess moisture, concentrating the meat's essence and creating a firm exterior that holds everything together.

This wasn't merely a cooking instruction but a demonstration of how God fashioned Israel as a nation. The Israelites weren't softened and dissolved by their Egyptian experience — they were hardened and strengthened by it. The fire of slavery, rather than weakening them, forged them into a cohesive people. Each challenge, each brick laid, each Egyptian decree against them only served to remove what was unnecessary and strengthen what was essential. By the time of the Exodus, Israel had been roasted by fire, not dissolved by water.

This pattern has repeated itself throughout Jewish history. The Egyptian slavery, the Babylonian exile, the destruction of the Temple by Rome, the Spanish expulsion, the Holocaust, and the wars since Israel's rebirth in 1948 have all served as the roasting fire that strengthens rather than dissolves. Each catastrophe that was supposed to finish the Jewish people instead concentrated what was essential to Jewish identity and survival. Rome destroyed the Temple and scattered the Jews across the world. The Jewish people outlasted Rome. Spain expelled its Jews in 1492. The Jewish people outlasted Spain. The Nazis murdered six million. The Jewish people responded by building a state.

October 7th followed the same pattern. When Hamas attacked, those same reservists who had threatened to refuse service reported for duty at rates exceeding 100%. Civilian volunteers flooded south to help evacuate communities and north to support farmers. Food banks overflowed with donations. The protests evaporated. The fractures closed. These aren't the actions of a people dissolving under pressure — they're the behaviors of a nation being roasted by fire, drawing together rather than falling apart.

Sinwar had studied the protests, the political divisions, the media coverage, and concluded that Israel was finally weak enough to break. He fatally miscalculated. The terrorists expected to find a fractured nation unable to defend itself. Instead, they encountered a people united by love of land, faith, and family. Israel's response confirmed what Passover teaches: when faced with existential threats, the Jewish people don't dissolve like meat in water; they solidify like meat in fire.

Passover isn't just a story we tell — it's our national DNA. Egypt's brutality forged the Jewish people in fire, not water. We didn't dissolve under pressure; we hardened into a nation. Walk through Jerusalem, Tel Aviv, or Hebron today and you'll find a people arguing fiercely yet standing together when it matters. Enemies have always mistaken our internal debates for weakness. They have always been wrong. History doesn't just repeat itself here — it confirms a biblical principle established the night we roasted a lamb and walked out of Egypt.

How the Jews Out-Godded Egypt

Shira Schechter

Four days before the Exodus, God gave the Israelites an instruction that must have seemed crazy.

Take a sheep. Bring it into your house. Tie it to your bedpost.

In Egypt, sheep weren't livestock. They were gods. To publicly parade one into your home and tie it up for slaughter was not a private religious act — it was a provocation. Every Egyptian neighbor who walked past could see what was happening. For four days, the Israelites sat with their sheep and waited.

Then, on the afternoon of the fourteenth of *Nisan*, they slaughtered them in broad daylight.

They painted the blood on their doorposts with hyssop and went inside. That night, the plague of the firstborn swept through Egypt. Every home with blood on the doorpost was passed over.

What made those homes different? The obvious answer is the blood as a sign. But Rabbi Immanuel Bernstein points to something deeper. The Israelites who performed this sacrifice weren't just marking their doors — they were making a declaration. By publicly rejecting what Egypt worshiped, they were choosing who they served. They were becoming, for the first time, servants of God.

This is why the Passover sacrifice carries such weight in Jewish law. Failing to bring it is one of the few positive commandments punishable by *karet* — divine excision, the severest consequence the Torah imposes. This isn't disproportionate. The Passover sacrifice wasn't just a ritual. It was the founding act of the Jewish people's relationship with God. Every year Jews brought it to the Temple, they were renewing that relationship, not just commemorating it.

The blood on the doorpost transformed the home. An ordinary entrance became something like an altar. The family inside had spiritually elevated itself above what was happening in Egypt around them. The plague didn't pass over them arbitrarily — they were protected because they had aligned themselves with God. The blood on the door wasn't a magic symbol. It was a declaration of allegiance.

This is the Exodus's deepest lesson. Freedom from Egypt was the precondition, not the destination. The real transformation was the choice the Israelites to belong to God, as God declared at Sinai: "I am the Lord your God who brought you out of Egypt to be your God" (Numbers 15:41).

The liberation was always for the sake of the relationship.

Physical freedom was the precondition. But what the Israelites discovered with a sheep and some hyssop, before they ever left Egypt, was something more important: that the deepest freedom is not freedom from a master, but choosing the right one.

The Bible's Wake-Up Call: Which Jews Will Merit Redemption?

Rabbi Elie Mischel

When I ask my son at dinner what he learned in school, he often answers with a groan: "We learned about the Exodus from Egypt – again!" I understand his reaction. We read this story twice daily in our prayers, we celebrate it during Passover, and we study it extensively when reading Exodus. It might seem like the most endlessly repeated part of the Bible (except for those detailed descriptions of building the Tabernacle!).

But this famous story is only repetitive if we're reading it wrong. While many view the Bible as either an ancient history book or a source of personal moral guidance, its purpose is far more profound. The Bible is eternal. It's the most contemporary book ever written, providing us with the divine lens through which we understand the events and challenges of our own time. When we read about the Exodus, we're not just learning about what happened thousands of years ago in Egypt; we're gaining insight into the patterns of redemption that continue to unfold in our world today.

"So God led the people roundabout, by way of the wilderness at the Sea of Reeds. Now the Israelites went up armed out of the land of Egypt." (Exodus 13:18)

The Hebrew word for "armed" – *chamushim* – can also mean "one-fifth." From this, the Sages teach that only one-fifth of the Israelites left Egypt, while four-fifths perished during the plague of darkness. This painful and shocking teaching raises two critical questions: First, what distinguished those who survived from those who didn't? What made some worthy of redemption while others remained behind? And second, what are the implications of this teaching for our own times? Which diaspora Jews of our generation will ultimately merit to leave America, England, and other countries and return to Israel and participate in the ultimate redemption of our people – and who, sadly, will be left behind?

The Sages explain the criteria for redemption: "Israel possessed three good attributes in Egypt, by whose merit they were redeemed: they did not change their names, they did not change their language, and they separated themselves from licentiousness."[14]

Rabbi Yehuda Leon Ashkenazi explains that these three traits that were necessary to qualify for redemption are not religious in nature, but rather national. These three attributes are the foundations of national identity. Hebrew names marked them as members of the Israelite nation. Their distinct language, Hebrew, bound them together as a people. And marriage within the faith ensured the continuation of their national story. Religious observance alone, while crucial, wasn't enough to guarantee inclusion in the Exodus. In order to be included in the redemption and leave Egypt, the Israelites had to identify themselves as part of the nation of Israel.[15]

This distinction between religious practice and national identity manifested itself in Jacob's encounter with his grandchildren in Egypt. When blessing Ephraim and Manasseh, Jacob first asked Joseph,

---

14. Bamidbar Rabbah 13:20

15. Sod Midrash HaToldot 8:304

"Who are these?" (Genesis 48:8). Clearly, Jacob already knew their names – they were his grandsons! Jacob was probing deeper, asking Joseph about his sons' identity. What he really wanted to know was, "Who are these boys, Ephraim and Manasseh? Are they Israelites at their core, or have they lost their Israelite identity and become Egyptians?"

The Bible is far more than a religious guidebook of commandments and prohibitions. The Jewish people are woven from three inseparable threads: the Bible, the nation of Israel, and the Land of Israel. Over the centuries, many Jews have come to identify with only one or two of these elements while neglecting the others. Some focus entirely on following the Bible's commandments, believing this alone makes them complete Jews. Others may feel connected to the Jewish people but remain distant from the Land of Israel. Still others may love the Land of Israel but see no need to follow the Bible's teachings. But Jewish identity cannot be parceled out this way – it requires all three elements. A Jew who keeps all the commandments but feels no connection to the Jewish nation or the Land of Israel has an incomplete Jewish identity. These divisions have created a crisis of identity that continues to this day.

I witnessed this confusion firsthand during a car ride with a young Orthodox Jewish man from New York. Despite his meticulous religious observance–his careful adherence to dietary laws, his daily prayers, his Sabbath observance–something was missing. As we discussed Israeli politics, he casually remarked, "You guys have such a crazy system here!" Those two words, "you guys," said everything. Here was a thoroughly observant Jew who saw himself as merely an American who practiced Judaism. He failed to understand that being Jewish means being part of the Jewish nation – Israel's problems are his problems, and Israel's destiny is his destiny.

Since October 7, we have witnessed a remarkable awakening of Jewish national identity. Consider Ginnifer Goodwin, a Jewish actress who had previously maintained only a distant connection to her heritage and to Israel. When asked to speak out about Israeli hostages, she faced a defining moment: "I was asked to post about the hostages, and my husband and I talked about it – 'What if I lose my career over this? What if I become some kind of pariah because I am standing up for us?' And it came down to this: 'We would be okay if we lost the house and had to pull the kids out from school.' The truth is, there's only one way this goes where I can sleep at night, and that's the way where I not only embrace Judaism, but I fight for the continuation of our people." Though far from religiously observant, Goodwin's powerful identification with the Jewish people marks her as worthy of redemption – for she understands that being Jewish means being part of Israel's destiny.

This awakening transcends all segments of Jewish society. Mendel Roth, an ultra-Orthodox Jewish singer, joined the Israeli military – a dramatic and unusual step for someone from his community. His song "I Run to Battle" captures this surge of national consciousness: "I heard I have a brother fighting for his brothers; Left behind both family and work for a whole year; I saw a heroic nation with a heart of gold; And I raised a flag, I'm running to battle." By embracing his role in the nation of Israel, Roth positions himself squarely among those who will merit to be part of the final redemption.

These aren't isolated cases. Across the world, Jews are rediscovering their connection to their people and their homeland. Just as in Egypt thousands of years ago, the key to redemption isn't found solely in religious observance – it lies in recognizing one's essential identity and true belonging.

This awakening might seem slow, but this is how redemption unfolds. Our role isn't to judge or grow impatient – it's to support and nurture this journey home. Those who see Judaism as merely a religion, divorced from national identity and the Land of Israel, risk excluding themselves from the redemption of Israel. The Bible isn't merely telling us an ancient story – it's illuminating the very path we walk today.

2

PREPARING FOR PASSOVER

Passover Then and Now

The dramatic events we've just explored—the plagues, the Exodus, the splitting of the sea—were not meant to be remembered as distant history. From the very first Passover in Egypt, God commanded that these moments be relived, retold, and reenacted by every generation. Yet the first Passover celebration in Egypt looked very different from how we observe Passover today. Over millennia, this foundational holiday has evolved through distinct eras, from its original observance in Egypt, through Temple-centered celebrations in Jerusalem, to its contemporary practice in Jewish homes worldwide. Throughout these transformations, Passover has maintained its core themes of faith, redemption, and divine providence while adapting to changing historical circumstances.

Passover in Egypt: A One-Time Experience

The very first Passover, known as *Pesach Mitzrayim* (the Passover of Egypt), was unique. It wasn't a commemoration of an event; it *was* the event itself. The Israelites were still enslaved, and their observance of these Passover commandments was an essential part of their redemption.

According to the sages,[1] the Israelites lacked sufficient merit to warrant redemption. They had lived for generations among Egyptian idolaters, absorbing their culture and practices. By giving them commandments to fulfill, God provided them with the opportunity to generate the merits they needed. These particular commandments also required them to publicly reject Egyptian theology and culture and align themselves with the God of Israel.[2]

God commanded each Israelite household to take a lamb on the tenth day of the month of *Nisan* and keep it until the fourteenth day (Exodus 12:3-6). This alone required tremendous courage, as the lamb was considered sacred by the Egyptians. On the afternoon of the fourteenth, the Israelites slaughtered these lambs and placed their blood on the doorposts of their homes. This served as a sign for God to "pass over" their houses when striking the firstborn of Egypt with the final plague: "And the blood on the houses where you are shall be a sign for you: when I see the blood I will pass over you, so that no plague will destroy you when I strike the land of Egypt" (Exodus 12:13).

The lamb was then roasted and eaten quickly, along with unleavened bread (*matzah*) and bitter herbs (Exodus 12:7-11). The people ate in haste, dressed as if ready to depart at any moment—because they were. That very night, Pharaoh relented, and the Exodus began.

---

1. Mechilta, Exodus 12:6

2. Rabbi Moshe Aberman, Pesach Mitzrayim, https://etzion.org.il/en/holidays/pesach/pesach-mitzrayim

Pesach Mitzrayim was a one-time commandment that prepared the nation for redemption. Through these acts of faith and courage, the Israelites generated the merit necessary for their liberation and declared their allegiance to God over Egypt.

Passover for Future Generations

Yet even as they observed that first Passover in Egypt, God commanded that this observance become an eternal memorial:

"This day shall be to you one of remembrance: you shall celebrate it as a festival to the Lord throughout the ages; you shall celebrate it as an institution for all time" (Exodus 12:14).

This ongoing Passover observance, known as *Pesach Dorot* (the Passover of the Generations), differed from the Egyptian original in several significant ways.

<u>The Paschal Offering:</u> In future years, the Passover lamb was no longer a hurried sacrifice performed in individual homes but a structured offering brought to the Temple in Jerusalem (Deuteronomy 16:5-7).

<u>No More Doorpost Blood:</u> In future Passover celebrations, there was no longer any requirement to mark the doorposts with blood.

<u>A Joyous Celebration:</u> Instead of eating in haste, with belts tied and sandals on their feet, the people of Israel were now to eat the meat of the Paschal lamb in a joyful, unhurried meal shared with their families, celebrating their freedom.

Expanded Commemoration: Unlike the first Passover in Egypt, later celebrations lasted seven days and included new practices, like avoiding leaven (*chametz*).

Teaching Children: Passover is not meant to be only a ritual but also an educational experience. Parents are commanded to actively retell the story of the Exodus to their children, ensuring that every generation understands the meaning of the holiday and the significance of freedom. As it says: "And you shall explain to your child on that day, 'It is because of what the Lord did for me when I went free from Egypt'" (Exodus 13:8).

Passover in Temple Times

When the Temple stood in Jerusalem, Passover wove together two distinct but inseparable observances.

"In the first month, on the fourteenth day of the month, at twilight, there shall be a passover offering to the Lord, and on the fifteenth day of that month the Lord's Feast of Unleavened Bread. You shall eat unleavened bread for seven days." (Leviticus 23:5-6).

On the fourteenth day of *Nisan*, Israelites from all the tribes converged on Jerusalem. The city filled with thousands of pilgrims, creating an atmosphere of unity and spiritual elevation. Each family or prearranged group brought their lamb to the Temple for sacrifice, where its blood was sprinkled on the altar. That evening, which marks the beginning of the fifteenth day of *Nisan* in the Jewish calendar, they gathered to eat the roasted lamb with *matzah* and bitter herbs, as their ancestors had done in Egypt.

But the observance didn't end with that meal. Beginning that same night and continuing for seven days, the Israelites entered what the Bible calls *Chag HaMatzot*, or the "Festival of Unleavened Bread," another name for the Passover holiday. During this week, no leavened bread could be eaten. The first and seventh days were designated as holy festival days of worship and celebration, when ordinary work was set aside (Leviticus 23:7-8).

The sacrifice marked the moment of redemption. The week-long festival commemorated the journey that followed.[3]

But why repeat this sacrifice year after year? Why not simply remember what happened in Egypt?

The Passover sacrifice, or *Korban Pesach*, was never just about remembering a past event. It was a statement: *I belong to the people of Israel.* The sacrifice of the first lamb in Egypt was an act of allegiance to God. The Israelites rejected the gods and values of their oppressors and committed themselves fully to the God of Israel. True freedom isn't only the absence of chains. It's choosing to follow God's values, even when they conflict with the surrounding culture.[4]

Every year, the Passover sacrifice renewed that choice. Bringing the lamb to the Temple was an active declaration of identity. It connected each family to the larger nation of Israel, reinforcing the shared story of liberation from Egypt and the ongoing covenant with God. Each

---

3. Shemot Rabbah 19:7

4. Rabbi Michael Rosensweig, *Korban Pesach: A Symbol of Faith and Commitment* www.torahweb.org/torah/2010/parsha/rros_bo.html

offering affirmed: *We are part of Israel. We are redeemed by God. We belong to Him.*

Passover Today

In 70 CE, the Romans destroyed the Second Temple, and the Jewish people were forced into exile. With the Temple gone, the Passover sacrifice could no longer be offered, and the annual pilgrimage to Jerusalem came to an end.

In the absence of the Temple, Passover is observed differently, yet its essence remains unchanged. While we can no longer bring the Passover offering, the first night of the holiday is still the highlight, as families gather for what is known as the Passover *Seder* (literally, "order"). The *Seder* combines symbolic foods, narrative, question-and-answer dialogue, song, and ritual to create a powerful multi-sensory educational experience designed to engage people of all ages and levels of understanding.

Emphasizing themes of freedom, gratitude, and faith, the *Seder* is structured around the *Haggadah* (literally, "the telling")—the text that recounts the Exodus and guides families through the rituals of the evening. A symbolic shank bone is placed on the *Seder* plate as a reminder of the Passover sacrifice. *Matzah* (unleavened bread) and bitter herbs are still eaten, as was commanded in Egypt (Exodus 12:8), and four cups of wine are drunk in celebration of redemption.

While we await the rebuilding of the Temple and the full restoration of the Passover offering, the *Seder* remains a powerful tool for transmitting faith, history, and hope from one generation to the next, a fulfillment of the verse: "And you shall explain to your child on that day, 'It is because of what the Lord did for me when I went free from Egypt.'" (Exodus 13:8)

Though the *Seder* is the main feature of the Passover holiday, the celebration continues for a full seven days[5] as commanded in the Bible (Exodus 12:14-20). The prohibition of *chametz* (leavened products) remains central throughout the entire holiday, requiring meticulous cleaning and preparation beforehand. This biblical commandment transforms the weeks before Passover into a period of intensive preparation.

Preparing for Passover

The weeks leading up to Passover are the most intense time of year in a Jewish home. Kitchens are emptied and scrubbed, special dishes are brought out from storage, and every family member joins in the meticulous search for hidden crumbs and traces of leaven. Preparation for the holiday is thorough and demanding—but it's also a time of shared effort and anticipation.

This annual ritual, which often becomes far more intensive than ordinary spring cleaning, transforms not just our physical spaces but our spiritual mindsets. At its core lies an ancient commandment: before

---

5. Outside of Israel, Jewish communities observe Pesach for eight days instead of seven. In ancient times, the new month was officially proclaimed from Jerusalem, but distant communities could not always receive the announcement in time to be certain of the correct date. To avoid celebrating the holiday on the wrong day, an extra day was added as a safeguard. This practice continues today in the Jewish diaspora.

we begin the Passover festival, all bread and leavened foods (*chametz*) must be completely removed from our homes and possessions.

The Biblical Foundation

The obligation to remove leaven from our homes is found in the following verse:

"Seven days you shall eat unleavened bread; on the first day you shall remove leaven from your houses, for whoever eats leavened bread from the first day until the seventh day, that person shall be cut off from Israel." (Exodus 12:15)

The prohibition of owning leaven is made even clearer in Exodus 13:7:

"Throughout the seven days unleavened bread shall be eaten; no leavened bread shall be found with you, and no leaven shall be found in all your territory."

Notice the two distinct prohibitions: you cannot *eat* leaven (*chametz*), and you also cannot *possess* it. Not in your home, not in your car, not in your office desk drawer. During Passover, *chametz* must simply not exist in your domain.

These verses set in motion the extensive preparations that define the season.

What Exactly Is *Chametz*?

Chametz refers to food made from one of five specific grains—wheat, barley, spelt, rye, and oats—that has been combined with water and allowed to ferment and rise. Think bread, pasta, cookies, crackers, cereal, and most baked goods. According to the Bible, any amount of *chametz*, even the tiniest crumb, is forbidden on Passover.

This explains why families spend weeks checking every corner of their homes.

But here's the fascinating contrast: *matzah*, the unleavened bread we *do* eat on Passover, is made from these same five grains! The difference? Timing. From the moment water touches flour, the dough must be kneaded and baked within eighteen minutes to prevent any fermentation. This strict process produces the thin, flat bread that symbolizes both the haste of the Exodus, when there was no time for bread to rise, and the humility of what the Torah calls *lechem oni*, the bread of affliction.

The Cleaning Process

Unlike regular household cleaning, Passover cleaning has a specific target: anywhere *chametz* might have been brought or stored. This focused approach helps families fulfill the biblical commandment without becoming overwhelmed.

The kitchen demands the most attention. Every surface, drawer, and appliance must be meticulously cleaned and then made kosher for Passover according to Jewish law. Countertops are covered. Ovens are heated to extreme temperatures. Metal utensils are immersed in boiling water. Dishes that touched *chametz* all year are packed away, and special Passover dishes are taken out from storage.

Dining areas require careful attention as pieces of food have a way of migrating between table cracks and behind chair cushions. Since these are the same tables and chairs where *matzah* will be eaten during Passover, they must be *chametz*-free.

Living spaces throughout the home need examination, especially anywhere people might have snacked during the year. Couch cushions often hide food underneath, and children have been known to stash snacks behind books, on shelves or in toy boxes.

Coat pockets must be checked for forgotten granola bars, as well as backpacks and lunch bags for old sandwiches. Purses and briefcases often have stray snacks stuffed in them. And for families with kids, the car needs a thorough vacuuming, since it's usually full of crumbs and forgotten food.

Not every area requires the same scrutiny. Places where *chametz* is never brought—like attics or dedicated storage areas—don't need special cleaning. And areas cleaned well before Passover, where food has not been brought, don't need re-cleaning. These distinctions help families focus their efforts where it matters most.

While eating even a tiny crumb of *chametz* is forbidden on *Pesach*, the requirement to remove *chametz* from your home focuses on quantities that are visible and accessible. Jewish law doesn't require perfection in cleaning—you're not expected to find every microscopic crumb that might be stuck in a crack or crevice. The goal is to scrub the areas where *chametz* is likely to be found and to ensure you don't knowingly possess or consume leavened products during the holiday. This practical approach prevents Passover preparations from getting out of hand while faithfully fulfilling God's command.

Joyous Preparation

The Sages teach that cleaning for Passover should be done with joy. This might sound strange when you're scrubbing the refrigerator late at night, but there's wisdom here. We're preparing our homes to celebrate freedom. Each drawer cleaned, each corner checked, is part of welcoming the holiday, and that is certainly joyous.

But joy is hard to sustain when you're exhausted. Families that spread the work over weeks rather than cramming it into the final days discover something important: the preparation becomes part of the holiday itself, not a frantic obstacle to it.

Bedikat Chametz: The Search for Leaven

After weeks of cleaning, the formal search begins. On the evening before Passover (the 14th of *Nisan*), Jewish families perform *Bedikat Chametz* - a ceremonial search for any remaining *chametz*. This rabbinic requirement ensures the biblical commandment to remove all leavened bread is properly fulfilled.

After nightfall, the head of the household recites a blessing over the removal of *chametz*, as this search is a fulfillment of the biblical command, "you shall remove leaven from your houses" (Exodus 12:15).

The search itself has a distinctive character. Using a candle (or flashlight in modern times), a feather, and a wooden spoon, one moves through the home looking for any remaining *chametz*. The candle's light reaches into corners and crevices that might otherwise be missed. The feather gently sweeps any crumbs found into the wooden spoon, which serves as a receptacle. These items—the crumbs, feather, and spoon—are then wrapped together and set aside to be burned the next morning.

Many families follow a charming tradition: ten pieces of bread are hidden beforehand to ensure the search yields results. Children often help hide these pieces, and then eagerly follow the searcher from room to room, watching as each piece is discovered and collected.

After the search concludes, a declaration is recited—a legal formula that nullifies ownership of any undiscovered *chametz*:

"All leaven and anything leavened that is in my possession, which I have neither seen nor removed, and about which I am unaware, shall be considered nullified and ownerless as the dust of the earth."

This declaration offers protection. If a forgotten piece of *chametz* is still hiding somewhere in the house, it no longer counts as yours. You've formally renounced ownership of it, so you haven't violated the biblical prohibition against possessing *chametz* on Passover.

Biur Chametz: Destroying the Leaven

The following morning brings the final step.

Before mid-morning on the 14th of *Nisan*—the time when it becomes prohibited to own *chametz*—any *chametz* found during the search, along with any other remaining *chametz* that you own, must be destroyed. This physical removal, called *Biur Chametz* (burning of the leaven), completes the process that began with the search the night before.

The *chametz* is traditionally burned, though any method that renders it completely inedible is acceptable. Many families gather together to watch as the *chametz* burns. Some use the moment to contemplate the symbolism; watching the physical bread consumed by flames serves as a reminder of removing spiritual obstacles from our lives.

As the *chametz* burns, a second, more comprehensive declaration is recited:

"All leaven and anything leavened that is in my possession, whether I have seen it or not, whether I have observed it or not, whether I have removed it or not, shall be considered nullified and ownerless as the dust of the earth."

This declaration is more extensive than the one recited the previous evening. It ensures that any *chametz* that may still exist—whether known or unknown—is nullified. The preparation is complete. *Pesach* can begin.

A Practical Solution

But what about expensive *chametz*? What if you have a collection of fine whiskeys or large quantities of grain products stored for the year? Destroying these would mean significant financial loss.

Jewish law provides a solution: *Mechirat Chametz*, the selling of the leaven. Jews sell their chametz to a non-Jew for the duration of Passover. This must be a legally binding transaction, usually conducted through a rabbi who acts as an agent. The *chametz* is stored in a specific location, sold before the holiday begins, and repurchased after it ends.

Why can Jews sell *chametz* to a non-Jew? Because God commanded the people of Israel, not all humanity, to remove *chametz* from their possession for the seven days of Passover. Non-Jews have no obligation to observe these laws. So when a Jew sells *chametz* to a non-Jew, that *chametz* is no longer in Jewish possession and the biblical requirement is fulfilled.

Over the years, many Jews and Christians have developed lasting friendships through this annual sale, and Christians who purchase *chametz* help their Jewish neighbors observe Passover. Some of these relationships span decades, renewed each spring as Passover approaches.

The Spiritual Meaning of *Chametz*

Why all this effort? Why such stringency about even the smallest crumb?

The sages teach that *chametz*, which rises and expands, symbolizes arrogance and ego. Just as *chametz* begins with the same ingredients as *matzah* but then swells with air, human pride begins with the same qualities as humility but becomes inflated with self-importance.

Think about it: flour and water mixed together become *matzah* if baked immediately, but become *chametz* if left to rise. The only difference is time and the introduction of air—puffiness, inflation, and expansion beyond one's true substance.

The process of removing *chametz*, then, becomes an exercise in humility, of removing the "puffiness" from our hearts. *Chametz* represents the inner enslavement that hinders true freedom. Just as the Israelites were physically freed from Egypt, we're called to free ourselves from the bondage of ego and self-indulgence.

Some commentators explain that *chametz* also symbolizes the evil inclination, which, like leaven, inflates our sense of self and distances us from our higher purpose. Removing *chametz* isn't just about physical preparation; it's about breaking free from the forces that hold us back from spiritual redemption.[6]

While we clean our homes from *chametz*, we're encouraged to simultaneously "clean" our inner selves. As we search for crumbs in crevices, we examine the hidden corners of our character. As we scrub away residue, we remove negative habits and traits that have accumulated over time. When we replace everyday items with those designated for Passover, we consider how we might replace ordinary mindsets with a consciousness of spiritual freedom and purpose.

The declaration we recite after searching for chametz contains a revealing distinction: "all the bread in my domain that I have seen and that I have not seen." On a deeper level, this refers to two different kinds of flaws. The sins "I have seen" are the faults we're aware of, the character defects we know we need to address. The sins "I have not seen" are the blind spots—the flaws in ourselves that we cannot see, or choose not to see. When we nullify the chametz, we're asking God to help us address both: the failings we acknowledge and the ones we're still blind to. No human being can do this work alone.

---

6. Rabbeinu Bechaye, *Kad HaKemach*

Special Torah Readings Leading to Passover

Preparing for Passover isn't just about cleaning cupboards and making kitchens kosher for Passover. In the weeks before Passover, synagogues around the world add special Torah readings to their regular Sabbath services, ancient texts that orient the community toward the themes of purification, redemption, and renewal.

Each of these readings addresses a specific aspect of preparing for Passover, both physically and spiritually.

Parshat Parah: Ritual Purification

On the Shabbat following the Jewish holiday of *Purim*, the Torah portion known as *Parshat Parah*, the portion of the Red Heifer, is read (Numbers 19:1-22). This passage describes one of the most enigmatic rituals in the Torah—the preparation of purification water from the ashes of a completely red heifer, used to purify those who had become ritually impure through contact with the dead.

Why read this now?

In Temple times, ritual purity was essential for bringing the Passover offering. Anyone who had become impure needed to undergo purification before participating in the Temple service or eating the Passover lamb. The purification process took seven days, which meant preparations had to begin well in advance of the fourteenth of *Nisan* when the offering would be brought. By reading *Parshat Parah* a few weeks before Passover, the community receives a public reminder: if you need purification, begin the process now. Don't wait until it's too late.

Today, without the Temple, the Passover offering cannot be brought, and according to Jewish law, we all remain in a state of ritual impurity—there are no ashes of the red heifer available to perform the purification ritual. So why continue reading *Parshat Parah*? Because the reading keeps alive the memory of these laws and the longing for their restoration. It's a statement of faith: we may not be able to perform these rituals now, but we study them, we remember them, and we prepare ourselves for the day when the Temple will be rebuilt, and these practices will resume. The reading isn't just historical nostalgia, it's active hope.

But there's a deeper dimension here. The ritual of the red heifer is famously inexplicable. Even King Solomon, the wisest of men, admitted he couldn't understand it.[7] The sages teach that this ritual represents the ultimate expression of obedience to God's will, even when we don't comprehend the reasoning. We perform it because God commanded it, not because it makes logical sense to us.

This theme resonates perfectly with Passover preparation. Just as our ancestors in Egypt demonstrated faith by taking a lamb—an Egyptian deity—and marking their doorposts with its blood, we demonstrate faith by meticulously following laws we may not fully understand. The preparation for Passover, like the ritual of the red heifer, requires us to submit to divine authority rather than human logic.

For nearly two thousand years, there had been no red heifers. The ritual described in *Parshat Parah* remained purely theoretical—studied, remembered, but impossible to perform. That changed in September 2022, when five red heifers were transported from Texas to Israel, the

---

7. Midrash Kohelet Rabbah 7:23

first time in nearly two millennia that such animals have been in the land for potential Temple use.

This remarkable achievement came through an unlikely partnership. When efforts by Jewish organizations in Israel to breed red heifers proved unsuccessful, a Christian organization called Boneh Israel stepped in to help. Christian ranchers in Texas had spent years developing pure red bloodlines specifically to help the Jewish people fulfill this biblical commandment. They understood the requirements and worked deliberately to produce heifers that would meet them. When the animals were ready, rabbis traveled to Texas to inspect them according to Jewish law, then coordinated their transport to Israel through this Christian-Jewish collaboration.

Though these particular heifers later developed disqualifying white hairs, the project's significance extends beyond the individual animals. It demonstrated that preparation for Temple restoration is not the concern of the Jewish people alone, but a shared mission with Christians who recognize Israel's prophetic role and are willing to invest their resources and expertise to advance God's purposes for Israel.

Now, when Jews gather in synagogues before Passover to read *Parshat Parah*, the words carry new weight. The infrastructure, expertise, and partnerships needed to fulfill this commandment have been established. What was once purely theoretical has become a documented possibility through unprecedented cooperation between Jews and Christians united in faith and reverence for Scripture.

Parshat HaChodesh: Sanctifying Time

On the Shabbat that falls on or immediately before the first day of *Nisan*, another special reading is added: *Parshat HaChodesh* (Exodus

12:1-20). This portion recounts what God told Moses and Aaron in Egypt two weeks before the Exodus. It begins as follows:

"The Lord said to Moses and Aaron in the land of Egypt: This month shall be to you the beginning of months; it shall be the first month of the year to you." (Exodus 12:1-2)

With this command, God was transferring to the Jewish people the authority to sanctify time itself.[8] The Israelite court would determine, based on witnesses who testified to seeing the new moon, when each month officially began. And since all the festivals are dated to specific days of specific months—Passover on the fifteenth of *Nisan*, *Shavuot* (Feast of Weeks) fifty days after Passover, *Sukkot* (Feast of Tabernacles) on the fifteenth of *Tishrei* (the seventh month)—the power to sanctify the new moon meant the power to determine when God's calendar would unfold.

Until this moment, the Israelites had no control over their own time. Slaves don't set their own schedules. Every hour belonged to Pharaoh, every day measured by taskmasters' quotas. Now, on the eve of their freedom, God gave them sovereignty over time itself.[9]

This reading also contains both the original command for the first Passover offering and God's declaration that this festival must be observed forever: "This day shall be to you one of remembrance: you shall celebrate it as a festival to the Lord throughout the ages; you shall celebrate it as an institution for all time" (Exodus 12:14). The Passover in Egypt wasn't a one-time event but the template for an

---

8. Rashi on Exodus 12:2

9. Sforno on Exodus 12:2

eternal practice. By reading this portion just as *Nisan* arrives, we're reminded not only of what our ancestors did in Egypt, but of our own obligation to observe Passover now — and to begin our practical preparations to fulfill it.

But there's something even deeper happening here. The medieval scholar Nachmanides points out that by designating Nisan as the first month, God was instructing the Jewish people to count the entire year from the Exodus. The months in the Bible are referred to by number, not name, and every month's number references redemption. When Jews say "the second month," they mean the second month after leaving Egypt. The third month is the third month after leaving Egypt. The calendar itself becomes a constant reminder of what God did.

This is similar to how Jews count the days of the week. In Hebrew, the days aren't named—they're numbered in relation to Shabbat. Sunday is "the first day toward Shabbat." Monday is "the second day toward Shabbat." Tuesday is "the third day toward Shabbat." This keeps Shabbat present in Jewish consciousness throughout the week.

Why does this matter? Because Shabbat testifies that God created the world in six days and rested on the seventh. By constantly referencing Shabbat, Jews continually acknowledge God as Creator. The same principle applies to the months. By numbering them from *Nisan*, Jews constantly reference the Exodus. Every time they mention a month, they're reminded that God redeemed them from slavery.

But why does a believing person need constant reminders of something they already know happened? Rabbi Israel Salanter, the nineteenth-century founder of the ethical self-improvement movement, taught a crucial distinction: knowing something intellectually is vastly different from internalizing it emotionally and allowing it to shape how we live. One of the most effective ways to move knowledge from the head to the heart is through constant repetition and contemplation. The Torah's numerous reminders of the Exodus—in the counting of months, in daily prayers, in Sabbath observances, in the festivals—aren't redundant. They're designed to ensure we don't just know about the Exodus as a historical fact, but that we internalize its lessons and see God's hand in our own lives.

But there is a more fundamental question that we need to ask. If Shabbat already reminds us that God created the world—surely the greatest miracle of all—why do we need this additional system of counting from the Exodus? Why isn't Creation enough?

The answer reveals something crucial about what the Exodus teaches us. Creation proves that God exists and that He made the world. But it doesn't necessarily prove that God remains involved in the world after creating it. Someone could theoretically believe that God created the universe and then stepped back, letting it run according to the natural laws He established, without further intervention.

Nachmanides explains that the Exodus proves something different: Divine Providence. It demonstrates that God doesn't merely exist as a distant creator—He remains intimately involved in human affairs. He sees suffering. He hears prayers. He intervenes in history. He cares about the fate of nations and individuals.

This is why the First Commandment doesn't simply say "I am the Lord your God" and stop there. It continues: "who brought you out of the land of Egypt, from the house of bondage" (Exodus 20:2). The Exodus is mentioned because it teaches an essential aspect of belief that Creation alone cannot convey: God's ongoing involvement in the world.[10]

By counting the months from *Nisan*, we're constantly reminded of this truth. Just as counting from Shabbat keeps the reality of Creation before us, counting from *Nisan* keeps the reality of Divine Providence before us. God didn't just make the world and walk away. He remains present, active, and engaged in our lives.

The prophetic reading that accompanies *Parshat HaChodesh* comes from Ezekiel 45:18-46:15, describing the Third Temple and the Passover offerings that will be brought there in the messianic era. The redemption that began in Egypt will reach its culmination in a future redemption—and by reading this passage now, we're reminded that the story isn't finished yet.

Shabbat HaGadol: The Great Sabbath

The Shabbat immediately before Passover carries a special name: *Shabbat HaGadol*, the Great Sabbath. But what makes this particular Shabbat "great"?

According to tradition, the first *Shabbat HaGadol* was the last Shabbat the people of Israel spent in Egypt—the tenth of *Nisan*, five days before the Exodus. On that day God gave the Israelites the extraordinary command for each family to take a lamb, tie it up, and keep it in their home for four days before slaughtering it (Exodus 12:3).

For the Israelites, this was terrifying. The lamb was sacred to the Egyptians. Slaughtering it would be blasphemy. And after 210 years

---

10. Ramban on Exodus 20:2

of slavery, many Israelites had absorbed Egyptian beliefs. Some probably worshipped the lamb themselves. Now God was asking them to publicly reject everything Egypt stood for.

Each Israelite family took a lamb—an Egyptian god—tied it up in their home, and kept it for four days while their Egyptian masters watched. Slaves openly possessing what their masters worshipped, preparing to slaughter what Egypt called sacred. It was an extraordinary act of faith, and it's why this Sabbath is called "great."[11]

Today, *Shabbat HaGadol* looks different but keeps its character as a day of preparation and anticipation. Rabbis traditionally deliver their longest sermon of the year, reviewing the laws of Passover. In the afternoon, many read through the *Haggadah* together, in preparation for the *Seder*.

The *haftarah* (prophetic reading) comes from Malachi and ends with these words:

"Be mindful of the Teaching of My servant Moses, whom I charged at Horeb with laws and rules for all Israel. Lo, I will send the prophet Elijah to you before the coming of the awesome, fearful day of the Lord." (Malachi 3:22-23)

The Hebrew word translated as "awesome" is *gadol*, or great. The "great" Sabbath before the first redemption foreshadows another "great" day—the final redemption that tradition teaches will also begin in *Nisan*, mirroring the Exodus from Egypt.[12]

---

11. Tur, Orach Chaim 430

12. Rosh Hashanah 11a

The Fast of the Firstborn

On the eve of Passover—the fourteenth of *Nisan*—firstborn sons fast from sunrise to sunset. This commemorates the fact that the Israelite firstborn were saved during the tenth plague, when God struck down all the Egyptian firstborn but passed over the Israelite homes (Exodus 12:29).[13] Although the plague actually occurred on the fifteenth of *Nisan*, it's forbidden to fast on a festival day, so the fast is observed the day before.

But this raises an obvious question: why fast to commemorate being saved? Salvation calls for celebration, not mourning.

The commentators offer different explanations. Some say the firstborn fast in mourning for what they lost. When God saved them from the tenth plague, they were designated for Temple service—a role of spiritual privilege and responsibility. But after the Sin of the Golden Calf, when the Levites stood firm while others worshiped the idol, God transferred Temple service to the tribe of Levi instead. The firstborn fast for the sacred role they forfeited.[14]

Others reach back to Egypt itself. According to this view, on the day before the plague struck, the Israelite firstborn fasted and prayed for God's protection, even though God had already promised they would be safe. Their fast wasn't about doubt—it was an expression of

13. Sofrim 21:3

14. Rabbi Shlomo Zalman Auerbach, Halichot Shlomo

humility and dependence on God in a moment of existential danger. The fast today reenacts what the firstborn did then.[15]

The fast applies to all firstborn males thirteen years and older. However, there's a widespread custom that releases them from this obligation. Communities hold a *siyum*—a celebration marking the completion of studying a Talmudic tractate or another significant Torah text—early in the morning. The joy of Torah study takes precedence over the fast. When participating in the celebration, the firstborn are released from fasting.

Ready to Begin

This brings the weeks of preparation to a close. The homes are clean, the kitchens are ready, and the laws have been reviewed. The special Torah readings over the past month have prepared the community. We've cleared our homes of leaven and our hearts are ready to experience freedom again.

In Egypt, families ate standing with staffs in hand, blood marking their doorposts, waiting for the moment they could finally run. During the Temple period, hundreds of thousands of pilgrims converged on Jerusalem with their lambs. Today, we gather in homes scattered across the world. The details have evolved. The night remains.

As darkness falls and the stars appear, Jewish families sit down together. The *matzah* is uncovered. The wine is poured. The youngest child will soon ask, "Why is this night different?" And once again, we'll tell the story: not as something that happened to someone else long ago,

---

15. Rabbi Yehuda Grunwald, Kol Bo Al Avelut

but as something that happened to us, that defines us, that continues to shape us still.

Collected Insights

An Officer's Holy Purchase

Sara Lamm

In the chaos of war, the most unexpected connections often emerge. During his service with the Nachal Brigade in Gaza, Rabbi Akiva Dovid Weiss developed a friendship with Hadi Falach, a Druze lieutenant colonel who commanded the army's Druze and Bedouin trackers. Their connection began simply enough—conversations over tea and coffee at Brigade Headquarters, moments of respite amid conflict.

During one such conversation, Hadi posed a question that caught Rabbi Weiss off guard: "Akiva, you're a religious rabbi, yes? So tell me, why is it that the Chief Rabbanite of Israel each year sells their *chametz* to a non-Jew who doesn't serve in the army? I'm an officer in the IDF, and I love and support the state and the Jewish people. How come they don't give this honor to purchase the chametz to someone like me? Can you arrange for me to be the one who purchases the chametz?"

For those unfamiliar, before Passover, Jews are commanded to remove all leavened products (*chametz*) from their possession. Since discarding large quantities of food would be wasteful, especially for businesses and institutions, Jewish law permits temporarily selling *chametz* to a non-Jew until after the holiday ends. This transaction, called *mechirat chametz*, is typically arranged through a rabbi who acts on behalf of the community. It's both a practical solution and a meaningful ritual that has taken place for generations.

What made Hadi's question so remarkable is that it goes beyond mere tolerance. He wasn't simply acknowledging Jewish practices; he wanted to actively participate in supporting them. In a world that often focuses on the minimum standard of peaceful coexistence, Hadi's request represents something far more beautiful.

Two weeks after their conversation, tragedy struck. Hamas detonated eight roadside bombs in an ambush. Four soldiers were killed, and six were wounded—including Hadi. As Rabbi Weiss helped with evacuation efforts, he found himself holding Hadi's hand as the wounded officer lay on a stretcher.

"Akiva, water. Please get me some water," Hadi requested.

Hoping to lift his friend's spirits, Rabbi Weiss responded, "Hadi, I'm not just going to get you water, I'm going to get you *mechirat chametz*!" Even in his pain, Hadi smiled and then laughed.

A few weeks later, when visiting Hadi during his recovery, the Druze officer hadn't forgotten. With a twinkle in his eye, he asked, "Nu, Akiva? What's with the *mechirat chametz*?" Rabbi Weiss laughed and told him, "I'm working on it!"

After reaching out to several rabbis without success, Rabbi Weiss took a chance and approached Rabbi Yosef Tzvi Rimon, the rabbi of Gush Etzion, asking for advice on how to fulfill this promise. To his complete surprise and delight, Rabbi Rimon responded: "We'll sell him all of the *chametz* of Gush Etzion!" Rabbi Rimon then had the Rabbi of Alon Shvut, Rabbi Vightman, contact Hadi to review the process, and arrangements were made for Hadi to purchase the community's chametz for Passover.

The ceremony to formalize Hadi's role took place at Tel HaShomer hospital, where he was recovering from his wounds.

The prophet Zechariah once envisioned a time when "ten men from nations of every tongue will take hold of every Jew by a corner of his cloak and say, 'Let us go with you, for we have heard that God is with you'" (Zechariah 8:23).

In a hospital room in central Israel, that ancient vision became reality. The question a Druze officer had asked over tea - "Let me go with you" - was finally answered.

The Timeless Tale of Freedom

Shira Schechter

The first commandment God gave the Jewish people came while they were still slaves in Egypt: "This month shall be to you the beginning of months; it shall be the first month of the year to you" (Exodus 12:1-2).

Before any other law, before instructions about food or worship or justice, God gave the Israelites control over their calendar. Slaves don't own their time. Their hours belong to their masters. By transferring authority over the calendar to the Israelites—making this month "to you" the first month—God was declaring: your time is now yours.

But ownership alone isn't freedom. The Israelites' first act with their newfound control over time was to use it for something sacred—the Passover offering. This is the difference between being free *from* something and being free *for* something.

We're not slaves in Egypt, but we can still lose control of our time.

We fill our calendars until there's no space left to breathe. We scroll through hours without noticing they've passed. We say yes to everything except what matters most. We mistake being busy for being purposeful.

Passover asks us: What are you doing with your freedom? Are you spending your days, or are you choosing them? Are you just marking time, or are you using it for something that matters?

A slave counts down the hours until work ends. A free person decides what those hours mean. But freedom without purpose is just emptiness with options. The difference between being free *from* something and being free *for* something is the difference between an open calendar and a meaningful life.

The *Seder* itself models this. We don't rush through the Passover meal. We linger over it. We tell stories, ask questions, sing songs. We turn an ordinary dinner into something meaningful by giving it our full attention and intention. The *chametz* we remove from our homes represents not just leavened bread but everything that puffs us up, distracts us, fills our time without filling our lives.

Think about what fills your days. How much of it expands to take up space without adding substance? How much of your calendar is *chametz*—impressive-looking commitments that leave you feeling empty? Social media scrolling that devours hours. Meetings that could have been emails. Commitments you said yes to because you couldn't say no. Busyness that looks productive but leaves nothing behind.

Passover preparation forces a reckoning. When you're cleaning out your pantry and finding expired food you forgot you bought, forgotten snacks shoved in corners, things taking up space for no good reason—that's not just about bread. It's about recognizing what we let accumulate in our lives without examining whether it belongs there.

The work of removing *chametz* is deliberate and thorough. You don't accidentally clean for Passover. You choose it. You schedule it. You make time for what matters by refusing to let what doesn't matter crowd it out. This is what it means to sanctify time—not just to fill it, but to choose what fills it.

As we prepare for Passover, we should ask: How are we using the time God has given us? Not just during Passover week, but every week. What would it look like to approach our calendars the way we approach our kitchens before Passover—searching out what doesn't belong, burning away what puffs us up, and making space for what actually matters?

Freedom isn't the absence of slavery. It's the presence of purpose. And purpose begins with the recognition that our time is both precious and ours to use wisely.

The Jews and the Moon

Rabbi Pesach Wolicki

"God said to Moses and Aaron in the land of Egypt: 'This month shall mark for you the beginning of the months; it shall be the first of the months of the year for you.'" Exodus 12:1-2

The opening verses of Exodus 12 introduce God's instructions to the Children of Israel regarding the preparations for the Passover lamb, leading up to the Exodus. God begins his words to Moses by telling him that the month in which the Exodus falls shall forever be known as the first month.

This does not mean that the counting of years would begin in that same month. Rather, that the numbering of months begins with the month of the Exodus. To illustrate, when we read later on in the Bible such verses as, "In the seventh month on the first day of the month, there shall be a day of rest for you" (Leviticus 23:24), the "seventh" month refers to the seventh month counting from the month of the Exodus, known today as the month of *Nisan*.

We should bear in mind that this counting of the months beginning with the month of the Exodus does not imply anything about the counting of years from creation. As is well known, *Rosh Hashana*, the Jewish New Year, takes place in *Tishrei*, half a year removed from the month of the Exodus. It may seem strange to people used to months and years being counted together, but the New Year begins on the first day of the seventh month. Again, this is due to the fact that the numbering of the months relates to the Exodus, not to creation.

The great Jewish commentator, Rabbi Abraham Ibn Ezra (1089-1167, Spain) points out that there is really no such thing as a lunar year, just as there is really no such thing as a solar month. Ibn Ezra goes on to explain that the cycle of the moon is slightly more than twenty-nine days long. The solar cycle is three hundred and sixty-five and one-quarter days long. Therefore, the concept of a "lunar year" is really just twelve lunar cycles. The natural cycles of the moon do not have a "year." Nothing significant happens to the moon every twelve months. Similarly, the twelve "months" of the three hundred and sixty-five-day solar year have nothing to do with the natural cycle of the sun. The months of the solar year we are familiar with, January, February, etc., do not reflect any natural phenomenon.

To sum up, for those who may be confused. The concept of a "month" is a lunar cycle, the full cycle of the waxing and waning of the moon. This cycle takes 29 and a half days. There is no "year" for the moon. A "year" is a solar cycle, the amount of time it takes for the Earth to travel around the sun. There are no "months" in this cycle. Nothing happens every 30 days or so in the solar cycle.

We are used to speaking of the Jewish calendar as a lunar calendar. This is not entirely accurate. As we explained, a purely lunar calendar would not have years. Rather, the Jewish / Biblical calendar is a lunar-solar calendar. We follow the lunar cycle to determine the beginning and end of each month. At the same time, we mark the years by counting twelve lunar cycles. This is the number of lunar cycles that comes closest to equaling the length of the year – i.e. one solar cycle.

Twelve lunar cycles equal 354 days. One solar year is 365 days. Due to this 11-day discrepancy, if left alone, the dates on a Hebrew calendar would be eleven days earlier each and every year. So this calendar can create a problem. The instructions for the festivals include the season of the year that they must fall within. For example, "You shall observe the Feast of Unleavened Bread—eating unleavened bread for seven days as I have commanded you—at the set time in the month of Abib, for in it you went forth from Egypt; and none shall appear before Me empty-handed" (Exodus 23:15).

Abib is the springtime, the time when the early grain begins to be ready for harvest. If the date of Passover was celebrated 11 days earlier in the solar cycle each year, it would not take too long for Passover to fall out in winter, then the fall, etc. To remedy this, Jewish law dictates that we insert an additional month every few years. This extra month readjusts the calendar so that the months will always remain in the correct seasons. To put it another way, most Jewish years have 12 months. Some Jewish years have 13 months.

The counting of months by the cycles of the moon has great spiritual significance in Judaism. Once a month, during the first half of the month – while the moon is in its growth phase – Jews will go outside at night and recite a blessing over the New Moon.

I'd like to draw attention to a few sentences of the liturgy that we recite at that time.

"May it be your will, Lord, to fill the moon so that there be no flaw in it. May the light of the moon be like the light of the sun and like the light of the seven days of creation, as it was before it was diminished, as it is said: 'The two great luminaries.' (Gen. 1:16) And may we fulfil the verse that states: 'They shall seek the Lord their God, and David, their king.' (Hosea 3:5) Amen."

We pray to God that this month, He should allow the moon to continue to grow past its size when it is full until it is the size of the sun. A moon that is the size of the sun would have no diminution in it. This is a strange request. What does it really mean?

The moon gives off no light of its own. The light of the moon is sunlight that is reflected to Earth. But the moon reflects only a very small percentage of the sun's light. When we only see a small sliver of the moon, only a small amount of sunlight is reflected down to us. The larger the moon, the more sunlight is reflected to Earth. When we pray for the light of the moon to be identical to that of the sun, we are saying that we want the moon to somehow reflect one hundred percent of the light of the sun. Only this way could the moon's light be equivalent to the light of the sun.

The sun is the source of light. The moon is the reflector of that light. God is the source of light. We, as servants of God, are supposed to act like the moon. As Jews, we see the moon as a metaphor for our mission. God is the light of good, morality, and truth. We strive to illuminate the world with God's light reflected through us to the world. Every time the moon renews itself, we see this as symbolic of another opportunity to increase the light of God in a world that is all too dark.

We pray that the amount of Godliness that we are reflecting grows and grows until it fills the world like the light of the sun in broad daylight. It is our fervent hope, prayer, and dream that we will somehow be able to so completely reflect God's light in the world that the world will come to a complete and pure understanding of God.

The *Chametz* Within and Without

Rabbi Elie Mischel

The thirty days between Purim and Passover mark a unique period in the Jewish calendar, centered on what Jewish tradition calls *biur chametz*—the elimination of leaven. During this time, Jews worldwide engage in the meticulous process of removing every speck of *chametz* (leavened bread) from their homes before Passover begins. This isn't merely spring cleaning; it's spiritual work encoded in ritual.

In Jewish tradition, *chametz* represents more than bread that has risen. The Hebrew word itself reveals its deeper meaning through its very letters. When we examine the spelling of *chametz* and *matzah*, we discover they share identical letters except for one: *chametz* contains the letter *chet* while *matzah* contains the letter *hei*. These two letters differ by only the tiniest gap—the *chet* is completely enclosed, while the *hei* has a small opening on its left side. This teaches us that *chametz* represents the ego that has closed itself off from God's influence, becoming self-contained and self-important. *Matzah*, by contrast, represents humility—remaining open to heaven's direction rather than being filled with self-aggrandizement.

The Torah states directly:

"No meal offering that you offer to God shall be made with leaven, for no leaven or honey may be turned into smoke as an offering by fire to God." (Leviticus 2:11)

God rejects *chametz* on His altar because it symbolizes ego inflation—human pride that has expanded beyond its proper boundaries.

Rabbi Eliyahu Dessler, the great 20th-century Jewish thinker, explains that *chametz* represents the evil inclination that causes a person to become puffed up with self-importance. Just as a tiny amount of yeast inflates an entire batch of dough, a small amount of ego can corrupt one's entire spiritual life. The thirty days between Purim and Passover are divinely designated for eliminating this spiritual bloat.

This work happens in three distinct phases:

First, *bedikat chametz*—the search for leaven. With a candle, feather, and wooden spoon, Jews search every corner of their homes for hidden *chametz*. This represents honest self-examination. What hidden pride lurks in the corners of our lives? Where have we allowed ego to take root? The Torah commands thoroughness: "Seven days there shall be no leaven found in your houses" (Exodus 12:19). The work requires looking in places we'd rather avoid.

Second, *bitul chametz*—the nullification of leaven. After the physical search, Jews verbally declare all undiscovered *chametz* to be "as dust of the earth." This represents the spiritual work of recognizing that whatever ego remains—acknowledged or hidden—has no real power over us. We nullify its claim.

Third, *biur chametz*—the burning of leaven. The morning before Passover, all discovered *chametz* is burned, completely destroying its physical existence. This is the final stage: not just recognizing our ego or diminishing its power, but actively eliminating it from our lives.

But this work isn't only personal. The principle of eliminating *chametz* extends beyond our individual spiritual lives to the broader world we inhabit. Just as we must confront ego in our own hearts, we must also confront evil when it manifests in the world around us.

Evil, like *chametz*, cannot simply be contained or managed. It must be thoroughly eradicated. The Torah's command regarding *chametz* is absolute: "none shall be seen among you" (Exodus 13:7). Not reduced. Not controlled. Not negotiated with. Eliminated. This same principle applies when confronting forces of murderous hatred in our world.

The prophet Obadiah foresaw this when he wrote:

"The House of Jacob shall be fire, and the House of Joseph flame, and the House of Esau shall be straw; they shall burn it and devour it, and no survivor shall be left of the House of Esau—for the Lord has spoken." (Obadiah 1:18)

Evil must not merely be contained; it must be eliminated.

King David understood this when he wrote:

"The wicked man schemes against the righteous, and gnashes his teeth at him. My Sovereign laughs at him, for He knows that his day will come." (Psalms 37:12-13)

Evil may inflate itself temporarily, but when confronted with truth and righteousness, its collapse is inevitable—if we have the courage to act.

Understanding these principles isn't enough. We must take decisive action. As we prepare our homes for Passover, removing every crumb of *chametz*, we're reminded that this work operates on multiple levels. We cleanse our own hearts of pride and self-importance. We confront evil in our communities and nations with the same thoroughness we apply to cleaning our kitchens. We trust that God, who redeemed our ancestors from Egypt, continues to work in history to eliminate evil and bring about redemption—but He calls us to be His partners in that work.

3

THE SEDER NIGHT

The Passover *Seder:* A Night of Freedom and Faith

How do you make a 3,000-year-old story feel immediate? How do you help a child in the 21st century understand what it meant to be enslaved in ancient Egypt? How do you turn distant history into personal experience?

The Passover *Seder* solves this problem brilliantly. It doesn't rely on words alone. It engages the senses—the taste of bitter herbs, the sight of symbolic foods, the sound of ancient songs. It structures the entire evening around questions. It gives everyone a role to play. And by the end of the night, each person has experienced something powerful: *I* was freed from Egypt.

The Torah commands us to teach our children about the Exodus "on that day." Not just to tell them the facts, but to help them feel the slavery, taste the bitterness, experience the liberation. This is why the *Seder* doesn't just recount history, it recreates it.

Every element of the *Seder* is carefully designed. Nothing is arbitrary. The foods on the *Seder* plate, the songs we sing, the questions children ask, the way we recline at the table—each detail creates meaning and memory. And woven throughout the evening are lessons about freedom, faith, education, and resilience that reach far beyond Passover night itself.

What Is a *Seder*?

The word *Seder* means "order" in Hebrew, referring to the carefully structured sequence of rituals and blessings that guide the night. Unlike an ordinary meal, the *Seder* follows a 15-step process, outlined in the *Haggadah*, the book that serves as the guide to the evening. Each step holds deep significance, leading participants from slavery to freedom, from suffering to gratitude, and from obligation to joyous faith.

The *Seder* is a blend of storytelling, song, prayer, and symbolic foods, all of which work together to bring the past into the present. It is designed to engage not only the mind but also the senses and emotions, ensuring that each participant, regardless of age or background, feels personally connected to the story of redemption.

The *Seder* Plate and Table

At the center of the *Seder* table sits the *Seder* plate, containing symbolic foods that tell the story of the Exodus:

***Maror* and *Chazeret*:** Bitter herbs, typically horseradish and romaine lettuce, that represent the bitterness of slavery that the Israelites experienced in Egypt.

Charoset: A sweet mixture of fruits, nuts, wine, and spices that symbolizes the mortar used by the Israelites to build structures during their enslavement.

Karpas: A vegetable, often parsley or potato, that is dipped in salt water to represent the tears of the enslaved Israelites.

Z'roa: A roasted shank bone which is symbolizes the Passover sacrifice that was offered in the Temple in Jerusalem.

Beitzah: A roasted egg, which represents the festival sacrifice (*Korban Chagigah*) brought on each of the three pilgrimage festivals—*Pesach*, *Shavuot* (Feast of Weeks), and *Sukkot* (Feast of Tabernacles).

Other essential items on the *Seder* table include three *matzot* (sheets of unleavened bread), often placed in a special cover or pouch, wine for the four cups drunk throughout the night, and a cup for Elijah the Prophet, who, according to Jewish tradition, visits every home on Passover night and will herald the coming of the Messiah and the ultimate redemption.

Matzah

Essential to Passover is *matzah*, unleavened bread. The Passover lamb was eaten with it, along with bitter herbs, as it says in Exodus: "They shall eat the flesh that same night; they shall eat it roasted over the fire, with unleavened bread and with bitter herbs" (Exodus 12:8).

But *matzah* isn't merely an accompaniment to the lamb. It carries its own significance, and is eaten throughout the entire seven-day festival: "In the first month, from the fourteenth day of the month at evening, you shall eat unleavened bread until the twenty-first day of the month at evening" (Exodus 12:18).

Matzah is bread in its most elemental form—just flour and water, mixed quickly and baked within eighteen minutes before the dough has any chance to rise. This mirrors what happened in Egypt: "And they baked unleavened cakes of the dough that they had taken out of Egypt, for it was not leavened, since they had been driven out of Egypt and could not delay; nor had they prepared any provisions for themselves" (Exodus 12:39).

But the Torah also calls *matzah lechem oni*, literally "bread of affliction" or "poor man's bread":

"You shall not eat anything leavened with it; for seven days thereafter you shall eat unleavened bread, bread of affliction—for you departed from the land of Egypt hurriedly—so that you may remember the day of your departure from the land of Egypt as long as you live." (Deuteronomy 16:3)

This raises a question that has bothered Jewish commentators for centuries: Does *matzah* symbolize slavery or redemption?

Some commentators see it as the meager fare of slaves: poor, rushed, and inadequate.[1] We eat *matzah* to remember what our ancestors ate as slaves in Egypt. This is reflected in the section of the *Haggadah* which beings: "This is the bread of affliction our fathers ate in the land of Egypt."

---

1. Nachmanides, Deuteronomy 16:2

Yet others see a problem with this interpretation. When the Israelites complained in the wilderness about their food, they remembered eating fish, cucumbers, melons, leeks, onions, and garlic in Egypt (Numbers 11:5), but not *matzah*. Apparently, even as slaves, *matzah* is not what they ate. Based on this, Rabbi Judah Lowe (1512-1609) maintained that they ate this unleavened bread for the first time on the night of their redemption.[2]

Matzah, then, represents something more profound than poverty. It captures the urgency of freedom—redemption arriving so swiftly that there was no time even for bread to rise. No taskmaster would be shouting at them in the morning. No quotas awaited them. They were leaving *now*, and there was no time to wait.

A Hasidic teaching captures this aspect of *matzah* beautifully. Rabbi Levi Yitzchak of Berdichev (1740–1809) asked his students: "Why does the Torah continually call Passover *Chag Hamatzot* (the feast of unleavened bread) while the Jewish people call it *Chag HaPesach* (the feast of Passover)?" His answer: "Because lovers emphasize each other's goodness. Israel praises God who passed over their homes when destroying Egypt. God praises Israel who trusted Him enough to walk into a barren desert with nothing but simple bread."[3]

So which is it, poor man's bread or bread of redemption? In truth, *matzah* embodies both realities. It's the bread of affliction that recalls suffering, and the bread of faith that celebrates redemption. Both truths coexist in those flat, simple loaves, making *matzah* the perfect

---

2. Maharal, Gevurot Hashem, chapter 51

3. Rabbi Levi Yitzchak of Berdichev in Kedushat Levi, *Derush le-Pesach*

symbol of a story that transformed slaves into a free people through courage, haste, and trust in God.

The Four Cups of Wine

Another feature of the Passover *Seder* is the drinking of four cups of wine at specific moments throughout the evening. This practice is rooted in the four expressions God used when promising to redeem Israel from Egypt:

"Therefore, say to the Israelites: 'I am the Lord, and I will bring you out from under the yoke of the Egyptians. I will free you from being slaves to them, and I will redeem you with an outstretched arm and with mighty acts of judgment. I will take you as my own people, and I will be your God.'" (Exodus 6:6-7)

Each cup corresponds to one of these promises:

V'hotzeiti - "I will bring you out"

V'hitzalti - "I will free you"

V'ga'alti - "I will redeem you"

V'lakachti - "I will take you as My people"

But why wine specifically? Why not water or another beverage?

Wine is a drink of royalty and celebration. In the ancient world, slaves didn't sip wine at leisure—they toiled under the lash. By drinking wine at the *Seder*, Jews physically enact their transformation from slaves to a free nation. Each cup becomes a declaration: We are no longer servants of Pharaoh. We are free.

The four cups also mark the progression of the *Seder* itself, creating a rhythm to the evening. They are drunk at the start of the *Seder*, after telling the story of the Exodus, after the Grace After Meals, and after concluding the songs of praise. Wine brings joy to each stage of the observance, transforming the recounting of ancient suffering into a celebration of redemption.

But if we look closely at the passage, God actually makes five promises, not four. The very next verse continues: "I will bring you into the land which I swore to give to Abraham, Isaac, and Jacob, and I will give it to you as a possession. I am the Lord." (Exodus 6:8) So why do we drink only four cups? Why isn't there a fifth?

Actually, there is. We just don't drink it.

Every *Seder* table holds a fifth cup that is poured but left untouched. It is called Elijah's Cup, named for the prophet who, according to Malachi, will herald the messianic age: "Behold, I will send you Elijah the prophet before the coming of the great and awesome day of the Lord" (Malachi 3:23).

According to tradition, Elijah travels from *Seder* to *Seder* on Passover night, visiting every Jewish home. After the meal, we pour his cup and open the front door wide, inviting Elijah in. And for just a moment, the boundary between the present and the messianic future feels thin. But the cup remains full.

The reason we pour but don't drink reflects where we stand in the story. The first four promises all concern the Exodus: leaving Egypt, breaking free from slavery, being redeemed with God's outstretched arm, and entering into a covenant relationship with God at Sinai. They describe a single dramatic moment in history — the birth of a nation. But the fifth promise reaches further. It speaks of a people finally home, dwelling securely in the land God swore to Abraham, Isaac, and Jacob. That is not just a chapter in the story. It is the destination the entire story is moving toward. And it is a promise still unfolding.

The *Seder* ends with the declaration "*L'shanah haba'ah b'Yerushalayim* — Next year in Jerusalem!" That cry is the fifth cup put into words. Four cups we drink, because four promises have been fulfilled. One cup we leave untouched, because the story isn't over. Redemption has begun. It is not yet complete.

Reclining

Beyond what participants eat and drink, even their physical posture at the *Seder* carries meaning. Participants don't simply sit upright at the table. When drinking the four cups of wine and eating *matzah*, they lean to the left in a posture of leisure and comfort.

This practice reaches back to the customs of the ancient world, where social status determined how you ate. Slaves stood to serve or sat upright while they hurriedly consumed their meals. Free people, especially the wealthy and aristocratic, reclined on cushions at banquets, leaning comfortably to one side as they dined at ease.

By reclining at the *Seder*, we physically embody our freedom. The body itself becomes part of the story. We don't just talk about liberation from slavery, we sit the way slaves never could. We eat and drink in the posture of free people, in the posture of royalty.

This seemingly small detail carries deep meaning. Freedom isn't merely a concept to discuss; it's a reality to be experienced with the whole self. Even our physical position at the table declares: We are no longer slaves. We recline because we can. We are free.

The Fifteen Steps of the *Seder*

The *Seder* unfolds through fifteen distinct steps, each with its own purpose and meaning. The Hebrew names of these steps create a memorable framework that has guided Jewish families through the rituals of the night for centuries, often sung to a traditional tune as each new step begins:

1. *Kadesh* – Sanctification The evening begins with *Kiddush*, the blessing recited over wine that sets the night apart as holy. This is the first of four cups of wine that will be drunk throughout the *Seder*. It is customary not to pour your own glass of wine, but to pour for the person sitting next to you—an expression of free people being served rather than serving themselves. The wine is then drunk while reclining to the left, in the posture of royalty and freedom.

2. *Urchatz* – Washing Hands A ritual washing of the hands, done without a blessing, preparing for the next step.

3. *Karpas* – Dipping the Vegetable A vegetable, often parsley or potato, is dipped into salt water, symbolizing the tears of the enslaved Israelites.

4. *Yachatz* – Breaking the Middle *Matzah* The middle of the three matzot is broken in half. The smaller piece is returned to its place, while the larger half is set aside as the *Afikoman*, a piece of *matzah* that will be eaten at the very end of the meal. This practice reflects *matzah*'s identity as *lechem oni*, poor man's bread. Just as a poor person breaks their bread and saves the larger portion for later, uncertain where the next meal will come from, so too does the *Seder* leader break and reserve this piece. The *Afikoman* is typically hidden for the children to find, a playful tradition that keeps children engaged and invested in the *Seder*.

5. *Maggid* – Telling the Story This is the heart of the *Seder*, when the story of the Exodus is recounted, fulfilling the Torah's commandment to retell the events of the Exodus. This section ends with the drinking of the second cup of wine.

6. *Rachtzah* – Washing Hands (Again) This time, hands are washed and a blessing is recited, in preparation for eating *matzah*.

7. *Motzi* – Blessing on the Bread The blessing over bread (*matzah*) is recited.

8. *Matzah* – Eating the *Matzah* A special blessing is recited over the *matzah*, and participants eat it while reclining. This is the fulfillment of the Torah's explicit command: "In the first month, from the fourteenth day of the month at evening, you shall eat unleavened bread" (Exodus 12:18).

9. *Maror* – Bitter Herbs Bitter herbs, traditionally horseradish or romaine lettuce, are eaten to recall the bitterness of the slavery. This fulfills the commandment given before the first Passover: "They shall eat the flesh that same night; they shall eat it roasted over the fire, with unleavened bread and with bitter herbs" (Exodus 12:8). The sharp, stinging taste brings the suffering of the Israelites into visceral experience. For a moment, those gathered at the table don't just remember slavery, they taste it.

10. *Korech* – The Hillel Sandwich A sandwich of *matzah* and *maror* is eaten, following the tradition of the ancient sage Hillel, who believed these should be eaten together along with the meat of the Passover offering.

11. *Shulchan Orech* – The Festive Meal A celebratory meal is enjoyed, featuring traditional Passover foods.

12. *Tzafun* – Eating the *Afikoman* The hidden piece of *matzah* is found and eaten. This is the last food consumed that night, leaving the taste of redemption on our lips.

13. *Barech* – Grace After Meals A prayer of thanks for the meal, including a blessing over the third cup of wine.

After drinking the third cup of wine, the door is opened to welcome Elijah the Prophet. According to Jewish tradition, Elijah travels from home to home on Passover night, visiting every *Seder*. A special goblet filled with wine is set for him at the table. As the door opens, participants recite verses invoking God's judgment upon the nations and welcoming the prophet who, according to tradition, will herald the coming of the Messiah and the final redemption.

14. *Hallel* – Songs of Praise Psalms of praise to God are sung, celebrating freedom and faith. The fourth cup of wine is drunk.

15. *Nirtzah* – The Conclusion of the *Seder* The conclusion of the *Seder* begins with a hopeful declaration: We have fulfilled the *Seder* according to its proper laws and customs. May we merit to observe it again—not in exile, but in the rebuilt Jerusalem. "*L'shanah haba'ah* *b'Yerushalayim*—Next year in Jerusalem!" What follows is a series of enigmatic and mystical poems, often sung to joyful, celebratory tunes that carry the evening into the late hours with song and praise.

Highlights from the *Haggadah*

The *Haggadah* contains dozens of prayers, songs, and teachings that guide the *Seder* from beginning to end. While every passage plays its role in the evening's progression, certain sections have become particularly well-known; either because they capture essential moments in the Exodus narrative, express core theological ideas, or have simply lodged themselves in Jewish memory through centuries of repetition. What follows are some of these key passages from the *Haggadah*, each offering a window into the themes and structure of the *Seder* night.

Ma Nishtana – The Four Questions

The *Seder* is built around questions. On this night, questions aren't just welcomed, they're required. The entire evening is deliberately structured to provoke them: strange foods, unusual rituals, behaviors that break from the ordinary.

At the beginning of the retelling of the Exodus story, the youngest child at the table stands and asks four questions that capture the strangeness of this night: Why do we eat only *matzah*? Why bitter herbs? Why do we dip our food twice? Why do we recline?

Mah Nishtanah - What Makes This Night Different

What makes this night different from all other nights?

On all other nights we eat either bread or matzah, but tonight there is only matzah?

On all other nights we eat any kind of vegetable, but tonight we will eat bitter herbs?

On all other nights we do not dip [our food] even once, but tonight we will dip it twice?

On all other nights we eat sitting up or reclining, but tonight we are all reclining?

These questions open the door to the story of the Exodus that follows. The answer begins immediately with a paragraph that starts with the words *Avadim Hayinu*, "we were slaves..."

Avadim Hayinu - We Were Slaves

We were slaves to Pharaoh in Egypt, and the Lord our God brought us out from there with a strong hand and an outstretched arm. If the Holy One, blessed be He, had not brought our ancestors out of Egypt, then we, our children, and our children's children would still be enslaved to Pharaoh in Egypt. Therefore, even if all of us were wise, all of us understanding, all of us knowledgeable in the Torah, we would still be obligated to tell the story of the Exodus from Egypt. And the more one elaborates on the story of the Exodus, the more praiseworthy it is.

This opening sets the tone for everything that follows. We don't just remember what happened in Egypt; we claim this story as our own. "We were slaves to Pharaoh." Not they. We.

That single word carries enormous weight. The *Haggadah* is not asking us to recall ancient history. It is asking us to inhabit it. As Rabbi Jonathan Sacks observed, on Passover night history becomes memory and the past becomes the present. You are not commemorating someone else's redemption. You are the person who walked out of Egypt. And had God not acted, you would still be there — and none of what followed would exist. No Torah at Sinai. No prophets. No Israel. Everything Jews have been and done across three thousand years of history traces back to that one night when God stretched out His arm and brought us out.

That is why the text doesn't stop at retelling. The more one elaborates, the more praiseworthy. Because this isn't a history lesson. It is a personal reckoning with the God who redeemed us — and on this night, we renew both our freedom and our bond with Him.

The Four Sons

The *Haggadah* recognizes that people engage with tradition in different ways. Since we are commanded to teach about the Exodus to our children, the *Haggadah* presents four types of children and how to respond to each:

The Torah speaks of four sons: one who is wise, one who is wicked, one who is simple, and one who does not know how to ask.

The wise son asks: "What are the testimonies, statutes, and laws which the Lord our God has commanded you?" You should explain to him all the laws of Passover, including the rule that nothing may be eaten after the Afikoman.

The wicked son asks: "What is this service to you?" To you—and not to him. By excluding himself from the community, he denies the essence of our faith. You should blunt his teeth and say to him: "It is because of this that the Lord did for me when I came out of Egypt"—for me, and not for him. Had he been there, he would not have been redeemed.

The simple son asks: "What is this?" You should tell him: "With a strong hand the Lord brought us out of Egypt, from the house of slavery."

As for the one who does not know how to ask, you must open the discussion for him, as it says: "And you shall tell your son on that day, saying: It is because of this that the Lord did for me when I came out of Egypt."

Each child receives what they need. The wise children get depth. The wicked get rebuke aimed at curbing their self-centeredness and reconnecting them to the community. The simple children gets clarity. And the silent children? They get an invitation into the conversation.

Rabbi Yosef Zvi Rimon offers a striking observation about the historical context of the wicked son's treatment.

The Bible tells us, "Now the Israelites went up armed out of the land of Egypt" Exodus 13:18. The Sages teach that the word *chamushim*, armed, in Exodus 13:18 shares a root with the Hebrew word *chamesh*, meaning five. Based on this linguistic connection, they explain that only one-fifth of the Israelites actually left Egypt. The rest, presumably wicked or lacking in faith, perished during the plague of darkness.

Therefore, the response to the wicked son implies that "had he been there, he would not have been redeemed." However, Rabbi Rimon emphasizes that this approach no longer applies in our time. After the Exodus, Jewish unity and mutual responsibility became central to our tradition. The concept is expressed in the Talmudic principle "All Israel are responsible for one another."[4] In our modern understanding, no one gets left behind, not even the "wicked" son. We are one people with a shared destiny and mutual responsibility. Rather than writing off those who distance themselves, we engage them, challenge them, and include them in our collective journey.

The traditional instruction to "blunt the teeth" of the wicked son takes on new meaning in this context. Rather than rejection, it suggests we must remove the sharpness and bitterness from his bite. We must smooth out his rough edges, heal his wounds, and allow the goodness in his soul to surface. Behind his wickedness lies a story, a reason why he allowed himself to become corrupted or jaded. We must identify the root cause and then neutralize it, reverse the process that led him astray, and bring him back to his inner goodness.

Had he been in Egypt, he would have gotten left behind. Not so anymore. Today, it is up to parents and teachers to engage these challenging children and try to uncover the hidden goodness within.

V'hi She'amda - This Has Sustained

Before recounting the Ten Plagues, the *Haggadah* pauses to acknowledge a sobering reality: persecution didn't end in Egypt. It continues throughout the generations. Yet so does God's deliverance. The words *v'hi she'amda*, "this has sustained us," refer to God's promise of redemption, the very promise that has sustained the Jewish people through their long and challenging history.

---

4. Babylonian Talmud, Shavuot 39a

This brief passage places the Exodus within the larger arc of Jewish history. Egypt was the first oppressor, but not the last. Yet the God who redeemed Israel from Pharaoh continues to preserve His people through every trial.

And it is this promise that has sustained our ancestors and us. For not only one enemy has risen against us to destroy us, but in every generation they rise against us to destroy us. But the Holy One, blessed be He, saves us from their hands.

The Ten Plagues

The Ten Plagues were the acts of divine power that broke Egypt and set Israel free. At the Passover *Seder*, we recite each one aloud:

1) BLOOD

2) FROGS

3) LICE

4) WILD ANIMALS

5) PESTILENCE

6) BOILS

7) HAIL

8) LOCUSTS

9) DARKNESS

10) FIRST BORN

When recounting the Ten Plagues, *Seder* participants don't simply list them. As each plague is named, they remove a drop of wine from their cup; a symbolic diminishing of joy in recognition of Egyptian suffering. This fulfills the principle in Proverbs: "When your enemy falls, do not rejoice" (24:17). The Egyptians deserved divine punishment for their cruelty and oppression. Yet even as we celebrate our redemption and acknowledge God's justice, we temper our joy in recognition that it came at a terrible cost to human life.

Dayeinu - It Would Have Been Enough

After recounting the slavery and the miraculous salvation from it, including the Ten Plagues, the *Haggadah* bursts into a song of gratitude called *Dayeinu*. The song follows the entire narrative arc of redemption—from leaving Egypt through receiving the Torah to entering the Land of Israel. Each verse isolates a single divine act and declares "*Dayeinu*!"—it would have been enough. If God had only brought us out of Egypt, that alone would have warranted our eternal gratitude. If He had split the sea but not given us the Torah, we would still owe Him everything. Yet God didn't stop at "enough." He gave abundantly, layer upon layer of blessing, and we owe Him gratitude for every single one.

How many levels of favors has God bestowed upon us!

If He had brought us out of Egypt and had not executed judgments against the Egyptians—Dayeinu! (It would have been enough!)

If He had executed judgments against them and had not destroyed their gods—Dayeinu! (It would have been enough!)

If He had destroyed their gods and had not slain their firstborn—Dayeinu! (It would have been enough!)

If He had slain their firstborn and had not given us their wealth—Dayeinu! (It would have been enough!)

If He had given us their wealth and had not split the sea for us—Dayeinu! (It would have been enough!)

If He had split the sea for us and had not brought us through it on dry land—Dayeinu! (It would have been enough!)

If He had brought us through it on dry land and had not drowned our oppressors in it—Dayeinu! (It would have been enough!)

If He had drowned our oppressors in it and had not sustained us in the desert for forty years—Dayeinu! (It would have been enough!)

If He had sustained us in the desert for forty years and had not fed us manna—Dayeinu! (It would have been enough!)

If He had fed us manna and had not given us the Sabbath—Dayeinu! (It would have been enough!)

If He had given us the Sabbath and had not brought us to Mount Sinai—Dayeinu! (It would have been enough!)

If He had brought us to Mount Sinai and had not given us the Torah—Dayeinu! (It would have been enough!)

If He had given us the Torah and had not brought us into the Land of Israel—Dayeinu! (It would have been enough!)

If He had brought us into the Land of Israel and had not built the Temple for us—Dayeinu! (It would have been enough!)

The word *Dayeinu* means "it would have been enough for us." Some interpret this as acknowledging that our merits were insufficient to warrant the next stage of redemption, yet God granted it to us anyway in His abundant mercy. We had not earned the right to progress further—not to the splitting of the sea, not to the manna, not to the Torah, not to the Land. Each additional blessing exceeded what our merits justified. Yet God gave freely, stage after stage, pouring out kindness far beyond what we deserved.

Pesach, Matza, and *Maror*

Rabban Gamliel, a leading Jewish sage and authority from the second century, established a fundamental requirement for the Passover Seder: whoever does not explain the following three things has not fulfilled their duty—*Pesach* (the Passover offering), *matzah* (unleavened bread), and *Maror* (bitter herbs).

Why these three specifically? Because together they encapsulate the entire story: the Passover offering recalls God's protection when He passed over Israelite homes in Egypt; the *matzah* represents the haste of redemption when there was no time for bread to rise; and the bitter herbs evoke the bitterness of slavery. These aren't just food; they are the essential elements of the Exodus narrative itself.

These items must be laid out before participants during the *Seder* so they can point to them as they explain their significance. Today, since the Temple no longer stands and the Passover offering cannot be brought, a roasted shank bone is placed on the *Seder* plate as a symbolic reminder. However, unlike the *matzah* and *maror*, which are lifted and shown, the shank bone is never picked up or pointed to directly—a precaution to ensure no one mistakes it for the actual consecrated offering or attempts to eat it as such.

It's not enough to talk abstractly about the Exodus. The story must be made tangible and real. We must see the symbols, speak the explanations aloud, and engage multiple senses in order to transform historical narrative into lived experience.[5]

Rabban Gamliel used to say: Whoever does not discuss these three things on Passover has not fulfilled his duty. These are: Pesach (the Passover offering), Matzah (unleavened bread), and Maror (bitter herbs).

Pesach—Why did our ancestors eat the Passover offering when the Temple stood? Because the Holy One, blessed be He, passed over the houses of our ancestors in Egypt, as it says: "It is a Passover offering to the Lord, who passed over the houses of the Children of Israel in Egypt when He struck the Egyptians and spared our houses" (Exodus 12:27).

Matzah—Why do we eat this unleavened bread? Because the dough of our ancestors did not have time to become leavened before the King of Kings, the Holy One, blessed be He, revealed Himself to them and redeemed them, as it says: They baked the dough which they brought out of Egypt into unleavened cakes, for it had not fermented, because they were driven out of Egypt and could not delay (Exodus 12:39).

Maror—Why do we eat this bitter herb? Because the Egyptians embittered the lives of our ancestors in Egypt, as it says: "They embittered their

---

5. Rabbi Yosef Zvi Rimon, *Shirat Miriam, Pesach Hagaddah*, p.110-111

lives with hard labor, with mortar and bricks, and with all manner of labor in the field; all their labor which they worked with rigor" (Exodus 1:14).

B'chol Dor Vador – In Every Generation

This paragraph is the theological heart of the entire *Seder*, the principle that transforms historical memory into lived experience:

In every generation, each person must see himself as though he personally went out from Egypt, as it says: "And you shall tell your son on that day, saying: It is because of this that the Lord did for me when I came out of Egypt" (Exodus 13:8). It was not only our ancestors that the Holy One, blessed be He, redeemed, but He redeemed us along with them, as it says: "And He brought us out from there in order to bring us to the land that He swore to our ancestors (Deuteronomy 6:23)."

This isn't a metaphor. It's a command to collapse the distance between past and present and to claim the Exodus as a personal reality. We don't observe Passover to remember what happened to someone else. We observe it because it happened to us. It defines our identity, our relationship with God, and our purpose in the world.

Shefoch Chamatcha – Pour Out Your Wrath

When the door is opened for Elijah, this stark prayer is recited:

Pour out Your wrath upon the nations that do not know You, and upon the kingdoms that do not call upon Your name. For they have devoured Jacob and destroyed his dwelling place (Psalms 79:6-7). Pour out Your fury upon them; let Your burning anger overtake them (Psalms 69:25).

Pursue them with wrath and destroy them from beneath the heavens of the Lord (Lamentations 3:66).

This is one of the most raw passages in the *Haggadah*. It voices the pain of a persecuted people and calls for divine justice against oppressors. It's a reminder that redemption isn't complete as long as evil persists in the world, and that ultimate justice belongs to God alone.

Hallel – Psalms of Praise

Towards the end of the *Seder* we recite *Hallel*, psalms of praise that celebrate God's deliverance. These same psalms were sung in the Temple and continue to be recited on Jewish festivals:

"Praise the Lord, all you nations! Extol Him, all you peoples! For His kindness has overwhelmed us, and the truth of the Lord is eternal. Hallelujah!" (Psalm 117)

"Give thanks to the Lord, for He is good, for His kindness endures forever." (Psalm 118)

The evening that began with questions and the recounting of slavery ends with unrestrained praise. This is by design. The Sages teach that the Passover story must be told by beginning with disgrace and conclude with praise.[6] From darkness to light, from bondage to freedom, from exile to hope—this is the arc of Passover, and of Jewish faith itself.

---

6. Mishna Pesachim 10:4

A Night to Remember

The Passover *Seder* is more than a meal; it's an immersive journey through Jewish history and faith. It connects generations, linking past, present, and future in a shared experience of storytelling, ritual, and reflection. Whether one is participating for the first time or the fiftieth, the *Seder* remains a night of discovery, meaning, and renewal.

As the *Seder* concludes with the words "*L'shanah haba'ah b'Yerushalayim*—Next year in Jerusalem!" we're reminded that the journey to redemption is ongoing. The Exodus was not just a one-time event but a promise that God's presence and guidance continue to shape the destiny of the Jewish people.

Collected Insights

Embracing Your Inner Child

Rabbi Elie Mischel

Have you ever walked with a child and had the following experience? You are on the way to school, or it is time to leave the park and go home. But whereas you are walking briskly, conscious of the time and where you have to be next, your four-year-old has stopped walking, completely mesmerized by an ant crawling out of a crack in the sidewalk. "Mommy – look!!" they yell with an intensity that matches your stress about being late to your next appointment. And at that moment, when you're caught between your own sense of urgency and your child's amazement, you have experienced the fundamental difference between adults and children.

Children experience the world in an inherently different way than we do. Rachel Sebba, an Israeli researcher, investigated the way children relate to the environment. Her findings prove what we already know anecdotally: that children experience the natural environment "in a deep and direct manner, not as a background for events, but, rather, as a factor and stimulator." Meaning, the things that we, as adults, no longer notice, the vast majority of the world which our minds no longer pay attention to, these are the things that children, with new fresh minds and a lack of worldly experience, will notice.

For example, children notice the cracks in the sidewalks, the bushes, the trees, and the pigeons. They see the clouds in the sky and count the stripes on your tie. As adults, we no longer see these things; but children do. What is background for us is front and center for our children! And they see these things with wonder.

Though adults and children most often experience the world very differently, on the first night of Passover, we are all supposed to be like children. How?

The meal eaten on the first night of Passover is called the *Seder*. At the *Seder*, we discuss the Exodus from Egypt in a question-and-answer format. The discussion starts with four questions, asked by the youngest children at the meal. It is so sweet to see the children nervously looking around, feeling shy, as they quietly begin to sing the four questions. These questions are new to them, and they often stumble over the words.

But if there are no children at the seder, Jewish law dictates that an adult must ask the questions. And if a person is having the *Seder* meal alone, he must ask himself the questions. Why must an adult ask questions they already know the answers to?

The answer lies in the fundamental difference between how children and adults experience the world. As we mentioned, children experience the world with wonder. In fact, when an adult experiences a moment of incredible wonder and amazement, the experience is called "childlike wonder." Wonder is, the phrase implies, the domain of children. To be a child is to question, to wonder, and to be amazed. Our children teach us how to see everything as if we are seeing it for the first time, without preconceived notions. Children understand, intuitively, how to see things with an open mind.

This childlike quality of wonder is at the foundation of science, and it strikes to the core of the religious personality as well. Rabbi Abraham

Joshua Heschel, a prominent Jewish thinker of the 20th century, believed that "wonder or radical amazement is the chief characteristic of the religious man's attitude toward history and nature. One attitude alone is alien to his spirit: taking things for granted, regarding events as a natural course of things."

The purpose of the *Seder* is to become children. One night a year we are commanded to stop moving, sit down at the table, talk about the awesome events of the Exodus from Egypt and be amazed! We mention the Exodus and the incredible miracles God performed for our people on a daily basis, many times a day. It is, therefore, inevitable that as adults these miracles should come to seem old hat. There is no way to escape it. And so, once a year, we are given the Passover *Seder* – an opportunity to shake ourselves out of adulthood and right back into childhood!

This explains the law that if there are no children at the table, or even if we are alone, we still must ask the four questions. Because on *Seder* night, we are obligated to be like children.

We spend most of our year as adults rushing, managing, and getting things done. The *Seder* gives us one night to stop. One night when we're commanded to sit at the table, ask questions, and wonder. One night to reconnect with our inner children. And maybe, if we do it right, that sense of wonder will last beyond the *Seder* table.

God's Blueprint for Passing Down Faith

Sara Lamm

Every year, as Passover approaches, I find myself doing what many Jewish mothers do: jotting down menus, assigning cleaning duties, debating which *kugel* (casserole) will earn a repeat performance. But alongside the brisket and the matzah ball soup, there's another list I obsess over — the stack of *Haggadot* I place at the table.

Because at my *Seder*, it's never just about retelling the story of the Exodus. It's about reaching the people gathered to hear it.

Let me be clear: the biblical commandments, the order of the *Seder*, the essential prayers and blessings – these remain unchanged. In Judaism, we call this *halacha* – the way we walk in obedience to God's law. These elements are non-negotiable and preserved intact across all *Haggadot*.

But within this fixed framework, the people who gather at my table are wonderfully different. There's the teenager who perks up only when the text connects to their experience. The Israeli cousin who craves something rooted in Hebrew. The questioning uncle who thrives on philosophical debate. The wide-eyed child who just learned to read and wants to feel important. And there's always someone new — someone who didn't grow up with the rituals, holding the *Haggadah* like it's both a map and a mystery.

I want to introduce you then to a tradition we have in my family. We use different types of *Haggadot* that engage different personalities.

There's the Hamilton-inspired *Haggadah* for the musical soul. The artfully illustrated *Haggadah* for the visually minded. The IDF *Haggadah* that reverently connects our ancient redemption to modern courage. One with scholarly commentary that digs deep. One with colorful pictures that welcomes the very young.

While these supplementary materials vary in presentation, they all conform to the essential required elements. It's not about changing the message – it's about ensuring the unchanging message is truly heard.

How can one story serve so many different hearts and minds?

The answer lies in the *Haggadah* itself, which gives us a model for this kind of tailored storytelling: the Four Sons.

"The Torah speaks of four sons: One is wise, one is wicked, one is simple, and one does not know how to ask." This ancient teaching comes directly from our *Haggadah* and is rooted in four separate passages in the Torah where God commands us to explain the Exodus to our children.

For the wise child, the Torah records: "When, in time to come, your children ask you, 'What mean the decrees, laws, and rules that *Hashem* our God has enjoined upon you?' you shall say to your children, 'We were slaves to Pharaoh in Egypt and *Hashem* freed us from Egypt with a mighty hand.'" (Deuteronomy 6:20-21)

This is the question of the wise child — he wants to understand the details, the laws, the full weight of our tradition.

For the wicked child, the Torah says: "And when your children say to you, 'What do you mean by this service?'" (Exodus 12:26)

He excludes himself from the community by asking, "What does this service mean to you?" We respond firmly about what God did for ME, not for him — showing that faith requires participation, not just observation.

For the simple child, the Torah provides: "And it shall be when your son asks you in time to come, saying, 'What is this?' that you shall say to him, 'By strength of hand the LORD brought us out of Egypt, from the house of bondage.'" (Exodus 13:14)

And for the child who doesn't even know how to ask, the Torah instructs: "And you shall tell your son in that day, saying, 'This is done because of what the Lord did for me when I came up from Egypt.'" (Exodus 13:8)

Each verse prescribes a different answer. A different approach. A different entry point into the same sacred story.

This isn't just good teaching technique. It's divine instruction. God Himself recognized that faith isn't transmitted through a one-size-fits-all approach. The Creator of all human personalities designed a transmission system as varied as the hearts receiving it.

This wisdom stretches far beyond Passover. It's about how we pass down any sacred truth.

In my home, I've seen children gravitate toward different aspects of our faith. One connects through music, another through study, a third through acts of kindness. Each finds their own gateway to the same God.

And I suspect this rings true for your families as well.

The genius of the Four Sons teaching is that it respects these differences without compromising the core message. We don't change the Exodus story — we change how we tell it.

This approach demands more from us as parents and teachers. We must know both our tradition AND our audience. We must be translators, making ancient wisdom accessible without watering it down.

Moses himself modeled this when he reviewed the Torah in the book of Deuteronomy, adapting his language for a new generation born in the wilderness. King Solomon understood this when he wrote, "Train up a child according to his way" (Proverbs 22:6).

And so I continue collecting *Haggadot*. Not because any single one is perfect, but because together they help me reach every person at my table. In their variety, they fulfill the true purpose of the *Seder*: not just to remember that we were slaves in Egypt, but to make each person feel as if they themselves had been liberated.

This is the miracle of successful faith transmission. Not that we say the perfect words, but that we find the right words for each listening heart.

Why are Eggs Eaten at the Passover Seder Meal?

Rabbi Pesach Wolicki

Every year, Jews around the world sit around the table as families and friends for the Passover *Seder*. We tell the story of the Exodus from Egypt, drink four cups of wine, eat *matzah*, and sing hymns of praise to God for His redemption of Israel, past and future alike.

During the long centuries of the Jewish exile, many customs were added to the Passover *Seder* by Jewish communities scattered across the globe. Many of these customs remain in practice only among those Jews who came from the lands where the customs began. Among the more peculiar customs is one that has been my favorite ever since I was a child. Many Ashkenazi Jews, those descended from European communities, will eat a hard-boiled egg just before the start of the main meal. The reason behind this custom is, at first glance, puzzling.

We find a discussion of this custom in the Code of Jewish Law known as the *Shulchan Aruch*, in a comment by Rabbi Moshe Isserles (1530-1572, Poland), who remains today one of the most influential codifiers of Jewish law:

It is customary in some communities to eat an egg as a sign of mourning. It appears that the reason is that the night of the Ninth of Av is established on the same night as the Passover Seder. Furthermore, we recall the destruction of the Temple because that is where the Passover offering was brought. (Shulchan Aruch, O.C.476)

The Ninth of Av, known by its Hebrew name *Tisha B'Av*, is the anniversary of the destruction of both the first and second Temples of Jerusalem. Remarkably, both Temples were destroyed on this same Hebrew calendar date over 6 centuries apart. To this day, *Tisha B'Av* is the national day of mourning for these tragedies. It is the saddest day on the Jewish calendar.

Rabbi Isserles tells us that the eve of *Tisha B'Av*, the beginning of the twenty-four-hour day of fasting and mourning, always falls on the same day of the week as the Passover *Seder*. For example, if the *Seder* is on Monday evening, *Tisha B'Av* eve will also be on a Monday.

Rabbi Isserles explains that because the Passover *Seder* and *Tisha B'Av* share the same day of the week, some Jewish communities have a custom of eating an egg.

Why an egg? In Jewish tradition, hard-boiled eggs are considered the food of mourners. For example, eggs are commonly eaten by the mourning family as their first meal after a funeral.

The pressing question we must ask about this custom is this. According to Jewish law, it is forbidden to show any signs of mournfulness on a festival. Even the practices of mourning for recently passed family members are suspended when a festival arrives. How is it appropriate to commemorate the destruction of the Temple on Passover, a time for rejoicing and praising God? Does the coincidence of the days of the week of Passover and *Tisha B'Av* warrant such a departure from the celebration of the festival? It's not like we engage in any kind of commemoration of the Exodus on the evening of *Tisha B'Av* as well. How are we to understand this unusual custom?

To answer this question, we must first know exactly when in the *Seder* this egg-eating custom is practiced. First, a brief synopsis of the order of the *Seder*.

After declaring the sanctity of the festival over a cup of wine, the *Seder* progresses through a few other short rituals to the telling of the Exodus story. After the telling of the story, the *Seder* moves to the eating of the ritually mandated foods, *matzah*—the unleavened bread—and *maror*—the bitter herbs. First, each of these is eaten alone. Then, the *matzah* and *maror* are combined in a sandwich and eaten together.

The basis for eating the *matzah* and *maror* together is a verse in the Bible from the instructions for the eating of the Passover offering.

"They shall eat the flesh that same night; they shall eat it roasted over the fire, with unleavened bread and with bitter herbs." Exodus 12:8

The word for "with" in this verse is *al*, which usually means "on" rather than "with." Based on this verse, the roasted meat of the Passover offering was eaten in a sandwich together with *matzah* and *maror*. Because we no longer have a Temple in Jerusalem and no longer bring the Passover offering, we are left with only the *matzah* and the bitter herbs. And so, we eat these two items together as a way of recalling what was done in Temple times.

After this *matzah* and *maror* sandwich is eaten, it is time for the main meal of the *Seder* to be served. And that is exactly when the custom of eating the egg is practiced.

Imagine that you are a Jew living at the time of the destruction of the Temple. In previous years, we slaughtered, roasted, and ate the Passover lamb at the *Seder*. Now there is no Temple. Passover has arrived. Imagine sitting at the *Seder* that night. For the first time in memory, we have a *Seder* with no roasted lamb. We tell the story. We arrive at the moment of the *Seder* when we would be eating the Passover offering. What are we going to do? We have no Passover lamb. Imagine now taking *matzah* and bitter herbs and eating them together for the first time without any delicious roasted lamb meat. What would be going through your mind as you ate this sandwich?

To illustrate this point, imagine being offered a hamburger. You gladly accept the offer. You are then given a hamburger bun with lettuce and tomato, but no burger. When you bite into this "burger" what is your first thought? There is no doubt that you would be thinking only one thought, "Where's the beef?"

The primary sensory experience is not of what you are tasting, but of what you are not tasting, of what is missing.

When we eat a sandwich of *matzah* and *maror* at the *Seder*, we are eating a roasted lamb sandwich without the roasted lamb. Like those Jews who sat down for that first Passover after the destruction of the Temple, we are supposed to taste what is missing, what is lacking. Without a Temple in Jerusalem, we are left eating a hamburger without the hamburger, a lamb sandwich without the lamb.

Now we can understand the custom of eating the egg. After telling the Exodus story and rejoicing in God's redemption, we take *matzah* and bitter herbs and eat them in a way that reminds us of what we are still lacking; the Temple in Jerusalem. In that moment, we literally taste the fact that God's temple lies in ruins. In that moment, we pause and mourn what is missing from the world and from our spiritual lives.

Even as we rejoice this Passover in God's salvation and redemptive acts in history, we must also take a moment to remind ourselves that we live in a broken world, and that we yearn for the day when we will once again give thanks and praise to God in the Temple in Jerusalem.

The Undetected Idol That Sabotages Your Faith

Rabbi Elie Mischel

When I served as a synagogue rabbi in New Jersey, I conducted a detailed survey of my congregation that revealed a troubling reality. The most consistent emotion my congregants experienced regarding their faith was failure and guilt. Behind the composed faces walking into synagogue every Shabbat, many hearts—young and old—were burdened by persistent feelings of inadequacy.

"There is so much more I should be doing," they confessed. "Why can't I avoid this sin, no matter how much I try?" Others lamented, "The Bible is so demanding, and I can never do enough." These weren't isolated sentiments but a collective cry I heard repeatedly across demographics.

This pattern troubled me. What begins as a holy desire to improve deteriorates when people see little progress. Guilt transforms into sadness and depression. After years of this emotional toll, resentment follows: "What do I need this for? Who wants a religion that just makes me feel bad about myself?" Finally comes emotional disconnection—people going through religious motions because social expectations demand it, while their hearts and minds retreat from engagement with God. And who can blame them? If your religion consistently makes you feel inadequate, disengagement becomes a survival mechanism.

Does believing in the Bible naturally lead to guilt? Is faith meant to be an endless cycle of feeling inadequate?

I rejected this interpretation utterly. I didn't want to be depressed. I didn't want my congregants to feel perpetually guilty. Such an existence isn't healthy—it's a tragic distortion of what the Bible intends. It's essential we understand why this attitude fundamentally misrepresents our tradition.

On Passover night, at the *Seder*, we read these words from the *Haggadah*, the traditional text that guides the Passover meal:

"*Mitchilah ovdei avodah zarah hayu avoteinu, v'achshav kirvanu HaMakom la'avodato*"—"In the beginning, our forefathers were idolaters. But now, God has brought us close to serve Him."

Rabbi Shmuel Weinberg of Slonim (1850-1916), a respected Jewish sage, offers a striking interpretation of this passage in his work *Divrei Shmuel*. He focuses on the Hebrew word "*Mitchilah*" (in the beginning) and explains that when a person constantly dwells on what they did "in the beginning"—their past mistakes and sins—they are like an "*oved avodah zarah*" (an idol worshipper).

This might initially sound like an exaggeration—how could dwelling on past mistakes be compared to worshiping false gods? But Rabbi Weinberg's point is precise: obsessing over our failures gives them more power than they deserve. It elevates our sins to a position they should not occupy in our spiritual lives. When we fixate on past failures, we often fall into despair and abandon serving God altogether.

The *Haggadah* text shows us a better way. The full passage reads: "In the beginning our fathers served idols; but now the Omnipresent One has brought us close to His service, as it is said: 'Joshua said to all the people: Thus said the Lord, the God of Israel, Your fathers used to live on the other side of the river – Terah, the father of Abraham and the father of Nahor, and they served other gods.'" The text acknowledges our ancestors' past failures—Abraham's own father was an idol worshipper, our people in Egypt sank to spiritual depths—but doesn't stop there. It immediately moves to the present: "But now, God has drawn us close to serve Him." This isn't merely historical narrative but a template for our own spiritual lives.

Yes, we all have our history of mistakes and failures. We don't ignore them—we face them and do our best to remove them from our lives just as we remove *chametz*, the leavened bread that during Passover symbolizes the puffed-up nature of sin and ego, from our homes. But then we affirm what matters most: "God has drawn us close."

The past is finished. Each person who genuinely repents from their sins and rededicates themselves to God is redeemed—set free. Now is the time to begin again, to start fresh and look forward to new growth.

"Fashion a pure heart for me, O Hashem; create in me a steadfast spirit. Do not cast me out of Your presence, or take Your holy spirit away from me. Let me again rejoice in Your help; let a vigorous spirit sustain me." Psalms 51:12-14

These words from King David capture the biblical path to renewal. After acknowledging his sin in the previous verses, David doesn't remain trapped in guilt. He asks for a clean heart and a renewed spirit—a fresh start unburdened by past failures. Most significantly, he asks for the restoration of joy. True repentance leads not to perpetual shame but to the recovery of spiritual joy.

The timing of Passover, the holiday of Spring, reflects this same principle. Just as winter gives way to new growth, our spiritual winters—times of sin and separation—can yield to spiritual rebirth. The symbolism is unmistakable: we are not meant to remain frozen in our past failures.

When we sin, when we fall short, we must respond with a healthy attitude: "I messed up. I wasn't able to overcome my natural inclination. I still have work to do. What can I do differently next time to be holier?" This approach—not endless guilt—is the key to joyous service of God, meaningful growth, and a healthy relationship with our Creator.

The Bible doesn't demand perpetual guilt but offers constant renewal. God desires our hearts, not our self-condemnation. What matters isn't how many times we've fallen, but that we keep rising, keep beginning again, keep turning toward God rather than away from Him. This is the true message of scripture—not a burden that crushes the spirit, but a path that liberates us to serve God with gladness, one new beginning at a time.

The Art of Questioning

Sara Lamm

We have a really fun Passover tradition in my family. It's purely silly, and as far as we know, it does not originate from an ancient ancestral book, nor has it been passed down for generations! But for as long as I can remember, my family has asked "The Four Questions," a hallmark of the Passover *Seder*, in as many languages as we know. Seriously. We've had people at our *Seder* table who have translated the text into every language from Spanish to French, Portuguese, sign language, and yes—the Star Trek language of Klingon. If you ever come to Israel and want to join our family Passover *Seder*, you've been warned: you might be asked to translate the Four Questions into an obscure foreign language.

But what exactly are the Four Questions? These are pre-written questions that the youngest member at the *Seder* table traditionally asks. They serve as the introduction to the section of the *Seder* where the story of Passover is told.

Here's what I want to explore: why do we open up the storytelling with questions? And what is the significance of asking questions in the Bible?

Those are great questions! And the answer reveals something essential about what it means to be free.

Think about it: slaves don't get to ask questions. When Pharaoh commanded the Israelites to make bricks, they didn't raise their hands and ask, "Why are we doing this?" or "Is there a better way?" Questioning authority was not an option. Questioning anything was dangerous. Slaves follow orders. Period.

But free people ask questions. Free people wonder. Free people probe and challenge and seek to understand. The very act of questioning is an expression of freedom.

This is why the *Seder*—the night we celebrate our freedom from slavery—is built entirely around questions. We don't just tell the story. We question it. We examine it. We turn it over and look at it from different angles. The Four Questions aren't just a ritual. They're a declaration: We are free. We can ask.

And here's the beautiful part: God Himself models this for us.

The Bible is filled with questions, and many of them come from God. The very first question in the Bible is God asking Adam, "Where are you?" (Genesis 3:9).

Is God asking for directions? Of course not. God knew exactly where Adam was hiding. He was asking Adam where he was internally. After eating the forbidden fruit, was Adam aware of what he had done? How did he feel about himself? God's question created space for Adam to reflect, to take ownership, to grow.

Similarly, when God asks Cain, "Where is your brother Abel?" (Genesis 4:9) the answer is obvious to God.

God knew what happened to Abel. But by asking Cain this question, He gave him an opportunity to reflect. God didn't say, "Cain! You terrible person, I know what you did!" He asked a question. He created space for Cain to confront his own actions, to potentially repent.

Cain didn't take the opportunity. He responded with his own question: "Am I my brother's keeper?" A question that revealed his refusal to take responsibility. But he *had* the opportunity. The question itself was a gift.

Now jump to the book of Exodus. Moses encounters something strange: a bush engulfed in flames that is not consumed. And Moses asks a question.

"Moses said, 'I must turn aside to look at this marvelous sight; why doesn't the bush burn up?'" Exodus 3:3

Moses could have walked past. He could have shrugged it off. But he didn't. He asked "Why?" And that simple question—that willingness to wonder about something unusual—set him on a path to encountering God and leading the Jewish people out of slavery.

Moses's curiosity didn't start at the burning bush. Earlier in Exodus, we see him observing the suffering of the Hebrew slaves.

"Some time after that, when Moses had grown up, he went out to his kinsfolk and witnessed their labors. He saw an Egyptian beating a Hebrew, one of his kinsmen. He turned this way and that and, seeing no one about, he struck down the Egyptian and hid him in the sand." Exodus 2:11-12

Moses looked. He noticed. He wondered why things were the way they were. And his questioning—his refusal to accept injustice as normal—was the beginning of redemption.

Questions lead to growth. Questions lead to understanding. Questions lead to change.

This is what we're teaching our children at the *Seder* table. When we give them the Four Questions to ask, we're not just preserving a tradition. We're giving them the gift of freedom. We're telling them: You have the power to wonder. You have the right to ask why. You can explore, challenge, and discover the world around you.

Today, as we navigate a complex world, this lesson matters more than ever. We live in an age where people are sometimes discouraged from asking real questions—where soundbites replace critical thinking, and where it's easier to accept what we're told than to dig deeper. This Passover, give your children the gift of questioning. Teach them how to ask, how to be curious, reflective, and inquisitive. Even if you don't have all the answers, you are unlocking their power to think for themselves.

At the *Seder* table, when we open with questions, we're doing more than reciting a ritual. We're affirming our freedom. We're modeling the kind of engagement with the world that God Himself demonstrates in the Bible. We're saying: This is what it means to be free. This is what it means to grow. This is what it means to live not as slaves who simply obey, but as people created in the image of God—people who wonder, who question, who seek understanding.

Or should I say, "¿Por qué?"

How to Build Resilient Faith

Shira Schechter

In February 2023, a terrorist drove his car into a crowd waiting at a bus stop in the Ramot neighborhood of Jerusalem. Six-year-old Asher Paley and his eight-year-old brother Yaakov Yisrael were killed. Their father, Avraham, was critically wounded. Their mother, Devorah, faced the devastating loss of two young sons while caring for her severely injured husband and their remaining children.

In the aftermath, Devorah Paley did something that stunned the nation. Rather than retreating into grief, she spoke publicly about her faith in God. Then, when the October 7th massacre occurred a year and a half later, she began visiting the newly bereaved families. A mother who had buried two sons was now offering comfort to others facing their own unimaginable losses. She became a source of strength for a traumatized country.

How? How does a mother who buried two sons maintain faith in God? And what does her answer teach us about how the Jewish people survived centuries of slavery in Egypt without losing their faith entirely?

The answer lies in a verse from Psalms 92:3: "To proclaim Your steadfast love at daybreak, Your faithfulness each night."

Rabbi Adin Steinsaltz explains that daybreak represents the good times—moments of clarity and blessing when God's presence feels obvious. Night represents the dark times, when we cannot see God's hand at work. The verse commands us to proclaim God's love in the morning *and* His faithfulness at night. Faith is not just for when things go well.

But where does faith in the dark times come from?

Devorah explained that the Hebrew word for faith, *emunah*, shares a root with *imun*—training. Faith is not just a feeling. It's a skill that must be developed through practice, like a muscle that grows stronger with use.

This is how the Israelites survived Egypt. They didn't simply wake up one morning after 210 years of slavery with their faith miraculously intact. They trained their faith. They spoke about God. They looked for His presence even in their suffering. They told stories of Abraham, Isaac, and Jacob. They passed down the promise that God would redeem them. By the time Moses arrived, their faith had been tempered by centuries of practice.

Devorah's father taught her another practice that strengthens faith: perspective. Every morning, Jews recite a blessing that God "decrees and upholds." On the surface, this means God upholds His own decrees. But her father explained it differently: When God decrees something difficult for us, He Himself is there to uphold us through it. The same hand that permits suffering provides the strength to endure it.

This shift in perspective changes everything. Do we view the tragedies in our lives as happening *despite* God—where was He when this happened?—or do we recognize that everything, both good and terrible, comes from Him? Those who cultivate faith in the good times see God's presence even in the darkness. Those who don't often spiral into anger and blame.

Devorah saw this firsthand when she visited bereaved families after October 7th. Families who had nurtured their faith before tragedy struck could access reserves of strength. Those who hadn't struggled with rage and despair.

This is why we train our faith before we need it.

At the Passover *Seder*, we recite a passage from the *Haggadah*: "In every generation, they rise up against us to destroy us, but the Holy One, blessed be He, rescues us from their hands." This isn't just historical memory. It's a statement of ongoing reality. The Jewish people have faced Pharaoh, Haman, the Romans, the Crusaders, the Inquisition, pogroms, the Holocaust, and now terrorists in Jerusalem. We have been enslaved, exiled, and massacred. But we have not been broken.

Why? Because like the Israelites in Egypt, we trained our faith. We practiced seeing God in the good times so that we can see Him the darkness. We proclaim His faithfulness each night.

Devorah Paley stands in that long tradition of those who proclaim God's faithfulness at night. Her sons' murders could have destroyed her faith. Instead, her faith—trained over years of prayer, study, and practice—carried her through.

This Passover, as we tell the story of the Exodus, let us remember that redemption required not just God's might, but the people's faith. That faith was not a gift. It was cultivated, practiced, and trained through generations of suffering. And it is that same faith, passed down through millennia, that sustains us still.

Is it Really Enough?

Rabbi Elie Mischel

Albert Einstein once said, "There are only two positions you can take. Either you believe that nothing in life is a miracle, or you believe that everything in life is a miracle." The Passover *Seder* is designed to teach us Einstein's second option: to see the miraculous in everything, even the ordinary blessings we take for granted.

One of the favorite songs sung at the Passover *Seder* is the song called *Dayeinu*, which means "It would have been enough." In this song we go through all the miracles that God performed for the Jewish people during the Exodus from Egypt and say that even if He had only performed that one miracle, it would have been enough. It would have been enough had God taken us out of Egypt, even without all the miracles. It would have been enough had God brought us to Sinai, even without giving us the Torah.

Of course, the obvious question about this song is "really?" It would have been enough? Obviously taking us to Sinai without giving us the Torah would not have been enough—we would have disappeared as a nation thousands of years ago had we not received the Torah!

What is the deeper meaning of this song?

The answer begins with a human tendency: we take for granted whatever we've always known. Alain de Botton, a popular British philosopher, observes that we live at a point in history in which our lives have been made incomparably easier than at any earlier point, due to a slew of incredible inventions. Electricity, washing machines, airplanes... the list goes on and on.

And yet, we find it almost impossible to be grateful for these life-changing inventions because it is rare to admire a technology which was already well established when we were children. Appreciation of the light bulb depends on having grown up with candles. Gratitude for the plane depends on having experienced travel on a steamship. De Botton suggests that we should track not only when inventions were introduced, but when they disappeared from our awareness through familiarity, becoming as commonplace as a pebble or a cloud.

If we take inventions for granted because we have grown up with them, we are even more likely to take for granted the most fundamental blessings of life: the food we eat, our bodies that function properly, and our family and friends that care for us.

Jewish tradition recognized this human tendency centuries before de Botton. Rabbi Bachya ibn Paquda (c. 1050–1120), in his book *Chovot HaLevavot*, gives a classic parable:

A man once found a boy abandoned in the forest and adopted him, caring for him like his own son. He fed him, clothed him, educated him and gave him everything he could possibly need. Growing up, the child, like any other child, took it for granted that his family would take care of him and love him.

Years later, the man who had adopted the child performed the great *mitzvah* of freeing a Jewish prisoner who had been kidnapped. The freed prisoner thanked him profusely and said "I owe my life to you for saving me! I could never thank you enough!"

In reality, the adopted boy was far more indebted to this man than the prisoner who had been freed. Whereas the man had performed one great act of kindness for this prisoner by paying to free him, he had done infinitely more for the boy! He raised the child from a young age, caring for him for years and years! And yet, the freed prisoner was much more grateful.

We, of course, are the ungrateful adopted son. Like the little boy, God cares for us every minute of every day. But we have grown accustomed to His kindness. Like electricity, it's old news and we no longer appreciate it. The problem is that while it may be human nature to take things for granted, appreciation of God's blessings is the foundation of the religious life. To be a religious person means to be a person who experiences awe; to be someone who appreciates.

Appreciating the kindness that God is constantly bestowing upon us is what compels us to serve God. By really looking at the world, by paying attention to the blessings of life, we are moved to want to repay God in some way, for all of His kindness. And so each of us is called to pay attention and to notice the blessings in our lives. By paying attention to the countless different blessings in our lives we overcome our inclination to be ingrates; we can slowly transform ourselves into thankful personalities, which is the very root of serving God.

This is precisely what the Psalmist calls us to do:

"Let them praise God for His steadfast love, His wondrous deeds for mankind." Psalms 107:8

Praise God for His wondrous deeds—not just the dramatic miracles, but the countless everyday wonders we've stopped noticing. This is why the daily prayers are saturated with reminders that stress the importance of thanking God, in specific ways, for all of the blessings of life both big and small. And throughout every single day, we make dozens and dozens of specific blessings: before and after we eat, after we use the bathroom, and more. Each blessing is an act of praise for a specific "wondrous deed."

And this is what the song, *Dayeinu*, is all about. *Dayeinu* is about learning to appreciate all the pieces of the puzzle; all the little miracles of life. *Dayeinu* is about being able to see the blessings that underlie the annoyances and struggles of life and learning to appreciate, in detail, all the goodness that we have in our lives. *Dayeinu* is about sitting at the *Seder* table and thinking about the countless miracles that had to fall into place so that each of us could be here today. *Dayeinu* is about counting our blessings, in detail, before God.

When we sing *Dayeinu*, we're training ourselves to see everything in life as a miracle—Einstein's second option. We're learning to notice what we've forgotten to appreciate. We're becoming the kind of people who can say "it would have been enough" for each individual blessing, because we've learned to see each one as extraordinary in itself.

Teach Your Children to Question

Shira Schechter

Every Passover, Jewish families around the world begin their *Seder* with a question asked by a child. "Why is this night different from all other nights?"

This isn't an accident. It's a deliberate educational strategy—and it reveals something essential about how Judaism passes itself from one generation to the next.

Most traditional cultures teach children through commands: "Do this because I said so." "Believe this because it's true." "Memorize this and don't ask why." The assumption is that children learn by accepting what their elders tell them without challenge.

Judaism takes the opposite approach. The Torah doesn't just permit children to ask questions—it commands parents to encourage them. In the section dealing with the Exodus, the Torah returns three times to the same theme: when your children ask, you must answer.

These passages became the foundation for the four sons in the Passover *Haggadah*. But they reveal something deeper: Judaism is transmitted through dialogue, not monologue. Through questions, not lectures.

Why does this matter?

Because facts memorized without understanding disappear in a generation. Commands obeyed without internalization crumble under pressure. But truths discovered through questioning become part of who you are.

Nobel Prize winner Isidore Rabi once explained how he became a scientist. While other mothers asked their children, "What did you learn today?" his mother asked, "Izzy, did you ask a good question today?" That one question shaped his entire approach to life. His mother wasn't teaching him facts. She was teaching him how to think.

This is what Jewish parents are supposed to do at the *Seder* table and beyond. We're not just passing down information about the Exodus. We're teaching our children how to engage with the world—through curiosity, investigation, and intellectual honesty.

Rabbi Jonathan Sacks noticed something remarkable: Hebrew has no word for "obey." When modern Hebrew needed such a verb, it had to borrow one from Aramaic. Instead, the Torah uses *shema*—which means to listen, to hear, to understand, to internalize, and to respond. Understanding comes before compliance.

This doesn't mean children shouldn't respect their parents or that boundaries don't matter. It means that Judaism values the development of the mind as much as the development of character. Maimonides called it the "active intellect"—the God-given ability to think, question, probe, and explore.

How do you create a home where children ask questions?

First, you have to welcome questions you can't answer. Some things we understand only with age and experience. Others require deep study. Some may be beyond us entirely. Even Newton admitted he was just "a boy playing on the seashore" next to an undiscovered ocean of truth. When a child asks a question you can't answer, say so—and explore it together.

Second, you have to model curiosity yourself. Children learn more from what they see than what they're told. If they see you wondering, questioning, investigating, they'll do the same. If they see you shut down inquiry with "because I said so," that's what they'll learn.

Third, you have to honor the question even when you don't like it. The *Haggadah* includes the wicked son precisely because some questions challenge us. But silencing uncomfortable questions doesn't strengthen faith—it teaches children that faith is fragile. Those confident in their beliefs don't fear hard questions.

At the moment Israel left Egypt to become a free people, Moses told parents to hand down the story to their children. But not through commands and lectures. Through questions. "Encourage your children to ask, question, probe, investigate, analyze, explore," Rabbi Sacks explained. "Liberty means freedom of the mind, not just of the body."

The *Seder* is designed as a teaching moment. The unusual rituals—dipping vegetables, leaning while eating, *matzah* instead of bread—are meant to provoke questions. "Why are we doing this differently?" The entire evening is structured around making children curious enough to ask.

But the lesson extends far beyond Passover night. Teaching children to question isn't just about one holiday. It's about raising thinking adults who can navigate a complex world, defend their beliefs with reason, and pass their faith to the next generation not through rote repetition but through genuine understanding.

This is how Judaism has survived. Not by building walls around the mind, but by training each generation to think. Not by demanding blind acceptance, but by inviting investigation. Not by fearing questions, but by making questions central to the entire educational project.

So the next time your child asks "Why?"—celebrate it. You're witnessing the mind doing exactly what God designed it to do. And you have the privilege of shaping not just what your child knows, but how your child thinks.

That's a gift that lasts far beyond childhood. That's how faith becomes more than inherited tradition—it becomes personal conviction. And that's how one generation successfully passes the torch to the next.

The Secret to Effective Parenting

Rabbi Elie Mischel

For years, parents have debated the most effective approach to raising children, with some advocating for tough love while others opting for a more nurturing approach. Amy Chua, also known as the Tiger Mom, contrasted the Chinese approach to raising children with the American one in her 2011 book Battle Hymn of the Tiger Mother.

Chua believes that children are far more capable than we give them credit for, and that we can't be afraid to demand more from them by pointing out their deficiencies and pushing them to their limits. She suggests that American parents are too concerned with their children's self-esteem and are hesitant to discuss their shortcomings, leading to an inability to handle failure.

On the other side of the educational spectrum, we find the "Self Esteem" approach to parenting, or as Richard Weissbourd, a psychologist at Harvard's School of Education, calls it: the "praise craze." Weissbourd says that by age 12, some children have been so overpraised that they regard compliments as implicit criticism. Other children, he says, become so dependent on praise that they are what he calls "praise sponges," becoming incredibly needy for affirmation.

What is the correct approach to parenting? Should we be more critical of our children, give them the honest truth about their abilities and effort and engage in more frequent discipline? Or should we focus solely on building up self-esteem and our kids' feelings of self-worth?

The answer, surprisingly, comes from the Passover *Seder*.

And you shall explain to your son on that day, 'It is because of what *Hashem* did for me when I went free from Egypt.' Exodus 13:8

The Sages tell us how we should tell the story of the Exodus from Egypt at the Passover *Seder*:[7]

"According to the understanding of the son, his father teaches him. He begins with disgrace and concludes with praise."

The sages of the Talmud explain that it is essential to discuss our spiritual and physical journey from idol worship and slavery to redemption and freedom. But why must we begin with disgrace? Why is it important to discuss the way we used to worship idols, or how miserable our slavery experience was? Wouldn't it be better to fully focus on God's miracles and His incredible salvation instead of mentioning the disgrace?

The fourteenth-century Spanish commentator, Rabbi Dovid Avudraham, suggests that the disgrace enhances and expands the praise. In order to deeply praise God for our good fortune, we need to understand and acknowledge the depths of how far we had sunk. We need to understand, and even re-live, slavery and exile in order to properly appreciate redemption. According to this approach, the disgrace has no inherent value, it is only necessary in order to make the praise more powerful.

I'd like to suggest a different approach that ties the disgrace and praise to the fundamental command of the *Seder* night: "You shall teach your children." The *Mishnah* says: "According to the understanding of the

---

7. Mishnah Pesachim 10:4

son, his father teaches him. He begins with disgrace and concludes with praise." This means fathers should teach their children by beginning with honest acknowledgment of challenges and ending with praise. When we teach our children we need to strike a healthy balance between acknowledging difficulties and celebrating strengths.

Like the Tiger Mom, we shouldn't be afraid to talk to our children about what they need to work on. We shouldn't practice revisionism or censor the reality of their mistakes. We must not be afraid to point out our collective errors, and we must not be afraid to point out to our children their challenges and where they need to improve. We don't avoid the "disgrace"—the honest reality of where they fell short or struggled.

But at the same time, we must also make sure to focus on our children's strengths and accomplishments and to highlight their successes. Even when beginning with honest acknowledgment of challenges, we must always try to finish the conversations with our children on a positive note in order to leave them with a good feeling and a strong self-worth! We begin with disgrace, yes, but we always finish with praise.

While the need to strike a balance between criticism and praise probably seems obvious, many of us still find ourselves constantly struggling to find that balance. For some of us, our children can do no wrong; they are the apples of our eye! The problem is that if we are not careful, our kids can become lazy and start to feel entitled. For these kinds of parents it takes real effort to acknowledge a little "disgrace."

But there are also some parents who excel at highlighting their children's (and spouses) faults and deficiencies. They are skilled at "disgrace," but these people need to work on making sure that all of their criticisms are expressed with love, and that they end with praise.

What the Sages teach us through their approach to the Passover *Seder* is that we need a healthy balance between discussing our children's shortcomings and encouraging them to achieve, while also highlighting their strengths and accomplishments. When we teach our children, we need to begin with "disgrace," but always end with praise, leaving them with a positive feeling and a strong self-esteem. By doing so, we can help our children develop the resilience they need to handle failure, and the confidence they need to succeed.

They Said It Then. They're Saying It Now

Shira Schechter

Growing up, Passover meant a table crowded with aunts, uncles, and cousins, singing songs and sharing Torah thoughts, and my grandfather—a rabbi—leading us through the ancient story of our freedom. But there was always one moment that stood apart from the traditional liturgy. After we opened the door for Elijah and recited the prayer calling on God to pour out His wrath on our enemies, my grandfather would add a prayer about the Holocaust. I was too young to grasp all the words, but one verse burned itself into my memory:

They say, "Let us wipe them out as a nation; Israel's name will be mentioned no more." Psalms 83:5

Even as a child, I understood that those words weren't just about ancient enemies. They were about something that kept happening, generation after generation.

Open the Bible, and you'll find the pattern repeating from the very beginning.

It started in Egypt. Pharaoh looked at the growing Israelite population and told his advisors, "Come, let us deal shrewdly with them, lest they multiply" (Exodus 1:10). His solution? Slavery. Oppression. And when that wasn't enough, infanticide—throwing every Hebrew baby boy into the Nile. The goal was clear: eliminate the Jewish people before they became too powerful.

We escaped Egypt, but the attacks didn't stop. At Rephidim, barely out of slavery, Amalek struck without provocation, targeting the weak, the elderly, and the stragglers at the rear of the camp (Deuteronomy 25:18). This wasn't a territorial dispute or a battle over resources. It was an assault on our very existence. God's response was definitive: "The Lord will be at war with Amalek from generation to generation" (Exodus 17:16). The Torah itself tells us this hatred would persist.

Centuries later, in the Persian Empire, the pattern resurfaces. Haman—identified as an Agagite, a descendant of that same Amalek—hatches a plot to annihilate the Jews. His decree? Destroy, kill, and annihilate all Jews, young and old, in a single day. The methods evolved, but the objective remained unchanged.

Even within our own borders, enemies conspired against us. Psalm 83 lists them by name: Edom, Ishmael, Moab, the Hagrites, Gebal, Ammon, Amalek, Philistia, Tyre, and Assyria. A coalition united by one shared purpose: Israel's destruction.

The biblical era ended, but the hatred adapted. Medieval Europe brought the Crusades, where mobs massacred entire Jewish communities in the Rhineland in 1096. The blood libel—the vicious lie that Jews murdered Christian children for ritual purposes—sparked waves of violence across Europe. England expelled all Jews in 1290. France followed. Spain's Inquisition tortured conversos, then in 1492 expelled every remaining Jew. Eastern Europe's pogroms brought organized massacres through Russian and Polish communities. The justifications evolved—religious fervor, economic resentment, political scapegoating—but beneath each new rationale lay the same ancient hatred.

Then came Kristallnacht. On November 9-10, 1938, Nazi mobs unleashed their fury across Germany and Austria. Synagogues erupted in flames. Jewish-owned businesses had their windows shattered. Thirty thousand Jewish men were arrested and sent to concentration camps.

The world expressed shock. Newspapers ran headlines. Diplomats issued statements. And then... the world moved on. Jewish communities swept up the broken glass alone, their cries for help fading into indifferent silence.

But Kristallnacht wasn't the end—it was the beginning. The Nazis claimed they were building a new world order, but their blueprint was ancient. Like Pharaoh, they feared Jewish influence. Like Amalek, they attacked without mercy. Like Haman, they sought total annihilation. The names and methods were modern, but the hatred was as old as Egypt.

Eighty-five years later, we heard those same words again: "Come, let us wipe them out as a nation."

On October 7, 2023, terrorists invaded Israeli communities, massacring over 1,200 people in their homes and at a music festival. Grandparents, parents, children, babies. They kidnapped hundreds, dragging them into Gaza. And in the aftermath, as Israel mourned and buried its dead, something chilling happened: across university campuses, city streets, and social media platforms worldwide, voices rose not in solidarity with the victims, but in justification of the massacre.

The ancient hatred that fueled Pharaoh's decree, Amalek's ambush, Haman's plot, the Crusades, the Inquisition, the pogroms, and the Holocaust is on the march again. Synagogues are being vandalized. Jewish students are hiding their identity on campus. Communities that thought they were safe are realizing they're not.

The psalmist wrote those words thousands of years ago, but they could have been written yesterday.

That prayer my grandfather added to our *Seder* wasn't just about remembering the past. It was about recognizing the pattern. He had lived through the era of the Holocaust, had lost family members in its flames, and he understood that the hatred didn't die in 1945. It went dormant. It waited. But it never disappeared. In fact, in the traditional Passover text, the *Haggadah*, we say, "In every generation they rise against us to destroy us."

But the *Haggadah* doesn't end there. It continues: "And the Holy One, blessed be He, saves us from their hands."

The same scriptures that document our persecution also promise our survival. After listing all the nations conspiring against Israel, Psalm 83 becomes a prayer for God's intervention: "Fill their faces with shame, that they may seek Your name, O Lord... Let them know that You alone, whose name is the Lord, are the Most High over all the earth" (Psalm 83:16, 18).

Throughout Scripture, we see this promise fulfilled. The prophet Jeremiah declared: "Thus says the Lord, who gives the sun for light by day and the fixed order of the moon and the stars for light by night... If this fixed order departs from before Me, declares the Lord, then shall the offspring of Israel cease from being a nation before Me forever" (Jeremiah 31:35-36). In other words: as long as the sun rises and the moon shines, Israel will endure.

Pharaoh's plan failed. We left Egypt not as scattered refugees, but as a nation. Amalek attacked, and we prevailed. Haman built his gallows and ended up hanging from them himself. The Crusaders passed. The

Inquisition ended. The pogroms ceased. The Nazis were crushed. The pattern of hatred is real, but so is the pattern of deliverance.

And here's what's different now: we're not sweeping up the broken glass by ourselves anymore.

After centuries of Christian persecution of Jews—from the Crusades through the Inquisition to the silence during the Holocaust—something remarkable is happening. Across the world, Christians are standing with the Jewish people, not just in words but in action. They're speaking out against antisemitism, supporting Israel, acknowledging the Church's historic role in Jewish persecution, and working to build a different future. What was once indifference has become partnership. What was once silence has become solidarity. Jews and Christians are crossing over the broken glass of history together.

My grandfather's prayer at the Seder table was his answer: Remember. Recognize the pattern. And refuse to be silent. He knew the hatred never truly died — it only waited. But he also knew what the *Haggadah* promises: "And the Holy One, blessed be He, saves us from their hands." This time, we don't face it alone. Jews and Christians are standing together, and the enemies of Israel will fail — as they always have.

4

The Week of Passover

The *Seder* night is over. The dishes are cleared, the children are asleep, and the house is quiet. But Passover is just beginning. What follows is seven days unlike anything else on the Jewish calendar — days that carry the story forward from the first desperate night of freedom all the way to the moment the sea closed over Pharaoh's army and Israel finally exhaled. This is the week that transforms an escape into a redemption.

The First Day

The majestic *Seder* ends, but Passover doesn't. The fifteenth of *Nisan* is a full festival day, carrying the same restrictions as the Sabbath. Work remains forbidden, and the family gathers again, this time for a festive daytime meal, with *matzah* replacing the braided *challah* that normally graces the holiday table. Wine is poured. The atmosphere is unhurried. After the intensity of the *Seder* night, the first day of Passover is a chance to breathe it all in.

In the synagogue, the morning service includes special Torah readings that continue the Exodus narrative, keeping the story front and center even as the dramatic night recedes. But one moment in the morning service stands apart: a prayer for dew.

In Israel, the rainy season ends right around Passover. The dramatic winter rains — the kind that drench the earth and fill the rivers — are over. What sustains the land through the long, dry summer ahead is something far quieter: dew. Each morning it settles silently across the ground, barely visible, yet nourishing everything it touches. On the first day of Passover, Jews formally make the transition in their prayers, shifting from requests for rain to requests for dew.

It's a small liturgical shift with a profound message. God doesn't always work through thunder and flood. Sometimes He works through what you almost don't notice — drop by drop, morning by morning, quietly sustaining a land and a people through the dry seasons of life.

The Intermediate Days of Passover

We've celebrated the *Seder*. We've observed the first day as a full festival. But Passover lasts seven days total, and most of those days fall into a category unlike anything else on the Jewish calendar.

To understand these days, we first need to see the Torah's framework for the entire week:

"Seven days you shall eat unleavened bread; on the very first day you shall remove leaven from your houses, for whoever eats leavened bread from the first day to the seventh day, that person shall be cut off from Israel. And on the first day there shall be a holy convocation, and on the seventh day a holy convocation; no work shall be done on them, except for what must be eaten for any person, that alone may be done for you." (Exodus 12:15-16)

The first and last days carry the full sanctity of a festival — set apart, holy, devoted entirely to spiritual celebration. But what about the days in between?

A Beautiful Paradox

Between the first and last days of Passover lies something curious: days that are simultaneously mundane and sacred, ordinary and holy. Jewish law calls them *Chol HaMoed*—literally, "the mundane part of the festival." The name itself is a paradox. How can something be both mundane and festive? How can days be simultaneously ordinary and holy?

This is precisely the unique character of *Chol HaMoed*. These intermediate days straddle the line between sacred and ordinary, creating a blend of holiness and weekday routine. They bridge the intense spiritual experience of the *Seder* and the climactic final day of the holiday.

Though they don't carry the full restrictions of the festival days, they're far from ordinary weekdays. Instead, they present an opportunity to continue celebrating, to embody the holiday's values, and to integrate the lessons of redemption into our daily lives.

Why Seven Days?

The Torah explicitly commands a seven-day celebration of Passover, but why? *Shavuot* (Feast of Weeks), which commemorates the giving of the Torah on Mount Sinai, lasts only a single day. Why does Passover require an entire week?

One answer lies in understanding that Passover reflects the full process of redemption, not just a single moment.

Passover isn't commemorating a single night. The first day marks the Exodus — God brought Israel out of Egypt. But the Israelites weren't yet free. Pharaoh was still behind them. The sea was still ahead. True deliverance didn't come until the seventh day, when the sea closed over Egypt's army and there was no going back. The week-long celebration traces that entire arc, from the first desperate steps out of slavery to the moment freedom became irreversible.

Freedom, it turns out, is a journey, not just a moment in time.

The sages saw something even deeper in those seven days. God created the world in seven days — but creation without purpose is an unfinished sentence. It was the Exodus, and the giving of the Torah that followed, that gave creation its meaning. By redeeming Israel and entrusting them with His law, God established a people who would bring His truth to the world. The seven days of Passover mirror the seven days of creation[1] — because in a profound sense, it was the Exodus that completed what creation began.

The Nature of the Intermediate Days

The partial sanctity of *Chol HaMoed* is reflected in Jewish law. While work isn't entirely forbidden, significant restrictions apply. The guid-

1. Shemot Rabbah 19:7

ing principle is simple: unnecessary labor should be avoided so we can focus on spiritual growth, family connection, and the joy of the holiday. And throughout all seven days, the prohibition against eating *chametz* remains absolute, reinforcing the unique spiritual character of the entire Passover season.

What May and May Not Be Done

What does this mean practically? What can you do on these days, and what should you avoid? The laws governing *Chol HaMoed* are nuanced. Broadly speaking, activities involving excessive effort that aren't essential for the holiday should be avoided. However, work that prevents financial loss, prepares food for the festival, or contributes directly to holiday enjoyment is generally permitted.

Activities typically permitted:

- Cooking and baking for holiday meals
- Travel for the sake of enjoying the festival
- Writing for necessary purposes (such as Torah learning or urgent business needs)
- Light work or craftsmanship, if delaying it would cause financial loss
- Taking care of medical needs

Activities typically prohibited:

- Regular weekday work, unless necessary for the holiday

- Laundry (except when clean clothing isn't available)
- Cutting hair and shaving (except in special circumstances)

These laws ensure that *Chol HaMoed* remains distinct from an ordinary weekday, preserving the festival's sanctity while allowing for practical needs to be met. The balance reflects the day's essential character—elevated above the mundane but accessible enough to maintain daily life.

The Joy of In-Between

Despite their in-between status, or perhaps because of it, the intermediate days are meant to be a time of joy and celebration. Many families take the opportunity to go on outings, visit relatives, or enjoy festive meals together. In Temple times, special sacrifices were brought on these days, a reminder that the entire week, not just its opening and closing days, are sacred.

Today, we honor the spirit of *Chol HaMoed* by setting aside time for Torah study, family bonding, and holiday fun. We find ways to celebrate without the full work restrictions of the festival days, but still acknowledge the sanctity of the season.

Chol HaMoed embeds a quiet but radical idea: holiness doesn't require withdrawal from the world. God isn't only present in the synagogue, at the *Seder* table, or on the Sabbath. He can be found on a family trip, around a lunch table, and in the middle of an ordinary afternoon. That is the spirit of these days — and perhaps one of the most accessible lessons Passover offers.

A Love Song for Passover

Of all the books in the Bible, Song of Songs is the most surprising. It reads as an intensely passionate love poem between a man and a woman, full of longing and desire. It doesn't mention God. It doesn't mention the Torah. On the surface, it has no business being in the Bible at all.

And yet Rabbi Akiva, one of the greatest sages in Jewish history, declared: "All the writings are holy, but Song of Songs is the Holy of Holies."[2]

Why? Because Jewish tradition understands this book not as a human love story but as the love story — the relationship between God and the Jewish people, told in the language of the heart.

During *Chol HaMoed*, on the Sabbath that falls within the intermediate days of Passover, Jews gather in synagogue and read Song of Songs aloud. The timing is deliberate. The Exodus, which we have just relived at the Seder, is understood in Jewish thought as the moment of betrothal between God and Israel — the engagement, full of the passion and intensity of new love. The prophet Jeremiah captures it: "I remember for you the kindness of your youth, the love of your bridal days, when you followed Me in the wilderness, in a land not sown" (Jeremiah 2:2).

Song of Songs is that love story told from the inside. The yearning. The devotion. The painful separations. The ultimate reunion. The relationship between God and Israel has never been smooth — there

---

2. Mishna Yadayim 3:5

have been betrayals, exiles, long silences. But the love has never broken. And it was on Passover that it began.

This engagement led ultimately to *Shavuot* (Feast of Weeks)— the giving of the Torah at Sinai, the wedding ceremony. The covenant wasn't a legal transaction. It was a marriage. And Song of Songs, the Holy of Holies, is its love song.

Counting the *Omer*

From the second night of Passover — the first night of *Chol HaMoed* — Jews begin counting. Not counting down — counting up, toward something. Toward *Shavuot*. Toward Sinai. Toward the wedding.

This daily count, called Counting the *Omer*, continues for seven full weeks, and it fulfills an explicit Torah command:

"And from the day on which you bring the sheaf of elevation offering—the day after the Sabbath—you shall count off seven weeks. They must be complete: you must count until the day after the seventh week—fifty days; then you shall bring an offering of new grain to the Lord." (Leviticus 23:15-16)

The word *omer* refers to a biblical measurement of grain (about forty-three ounces), which in Temple times was brought as an offering on the second day of Passover. This was a wave offering of barley, harvested the night before and brought to the Temple along with a lamb. Fifty days later, on *Shavuot*, another grain offering was brought, this time from the new wheat harvest. The counting connected these two offerings, bridging the spring barley harvest and the summer wheat harvest.

But the counting connects something far more significant than agricultural seasons.

According to Jewish tradition, these forty-nine days mark the journey from Egypt to Sinai—from physical liberation to spiritual purpose. The Israelites left Egypt on Passover. Seven weeks later, they stood at the foot of Mount Sinai and received the Torah. The counting reflects this progression: we count up, not down, because we're moving toward something. Each day brings us closer to Sinai.

Passover gives us freedom *from* something. *Shavuot* gives us freedom *for* something. The *Omer* period is the bridge between these two realities—the time when slaves become a nation with a divine mission.

This daily ritual, repeated for seven weeks, turns the intermediate days of Passover into the beginning of a longer journey. We don't just celebrate our freedom for a week and then return to ordinary life. We count. We measure. We march deliberately toward Sinai, acknowledging that redemption isn't complete until we accept the purpose for which we were redeemed.

The Final Day of Passover

For six days, we've been celebrating freedom. But six days after leaving Egypt, the Israelites were not yet safe. Pharaoh had a change of heart, and his army was coming after them.

The seventh day of Passover is when the story reaches its climax.

The Bible commands that this final day, like the first, be observed as "a holy convocation; no work shall be done" (Exodus 12:16). We're still forbidden to eat *chametz*. We're still in Passover. But this day carries its own significance. If the first day marks the exodus from Egypt, the seventh day marks the moment Egypt could no longer pursue the Israelites. Freedom wasn't secure until the sea closed over Pharaoh's army.

The Splitting of the Sea: Complete Redemption

The Jewish people, newly freed from Egyptian slavery, had marched into the wilderness with faith in God's promise. But just seven days after their departure, they found themselves trapped.

Before them lay the sea. Behind them, the might of Pharaoh's army: chariots and warriors determined to force them back into servitude.

At that moment of crisis, fear threatened to overtake them. Some cried out in despair. Others wished to surrender. But God's command to Moses was clear:

"Why do you cry out to Me? Speak to the children of Israel, and let them journey forth." (Exodus 14:15)

Moses raised his staff. God caused a mighty east wind to blow all night. The sea parted, its waters forming towering walls on either side, and the Israelites crossed on dry land. When Pharaoh's army pursued them, the waters returned to their natural state, drowning the Egyptians and delivering the Jewish people from their grasp once and for all.

The seventh day of Passover celebrates this miracle and the culmination of the Exodus. The first and seventh days, each celebrated as full festival days, commemorate different stages of physical redemption:

the first day marks the beginning, the seventh day marks the completion.

Why does the Splitting of the Sea mark the completion of freedom? Because only at that moment did the Jewish people become truly free. Until then, they still saw themselves as subjects of Egypt. But once they witnessed their former oppressors drowned in the sea, they finally experienced complete liberation.

A Revelation Like No Other

In addition to physical freedom, the sages teach that at the Splitting of the Sea, even the simplest maidservant saw a level of divine revelation greater than that of the prophet Ezekiel.[3]

Consider that for a moment. Ezekiel's visions, including the mystical chapters of the Divine Chariot, are among the most esoteric and profound in the entire Bible. And yet, what he struggled to perceive, the Jewish people—every man, woman, and child—witnessed with absolute clarity at the sea.

This was a moment of complete divine presence. Even those of the lowest social status were granted prophetic insight beyond the greatest prophets of later generations.

The redemption at the sea wasn't just physical salvation; it was an unparalleled spiritual experience that left an everlasting imprint on the Jewish people. "And when Israel saw the wondrous power that God

---

3. *Mechilta*, *Beshalach* 3

had wielded against the Egyptians, the people feared God; they had faith in God and in Moses—God's servant" (Exodus 14:31).

The Splitting of the Sea revealed God's boundless power, His intimate involvement in their fate, and confirmed that their journey to freedom was guided by divine will.

Faith Leads to Action

Yet this revelation didn't come passively. It required action driven by faith, even before the miracle occurred.

This lesson is exemplified in the story of Nahshon, son of Amminadab, a prince of the tribe of Judah. According to tradition, as the Israelites stood at the edge of the sea with the Egyptian army closing in behind them, fear and hesitation gripped the people. While some cried out in despair and others debated what to do, Nahshon took action.

Nahshon didn't wait for divine intervention. He stepped into the water, walking forward with unwavering faith.[4] He waded deeper and deeper—up to his knees, his waist, his shoulders—until the waves reached his nose. Only at that moment, when he demonstrated complete trust in God's promise, did the sea split before him, revealing the dry land upon which the Israelites would walk to freedom.

Nahshon's boldness teaches a crucial truth: redemption requires action. Miracles don't always precede faith; often, faith must come first. The Jewish people weren't meant to wait passively for salvation; they had to take the first step forward, even when the way was uncertain.

4. Babylonian Talmud, Sotah 37a

The last day of Passover carries unique spiritual significance. It reminds us that divine redemption isn't only about God's intervention in history but about our willingness to trust, to step forward, and to believe that even when the path ahead seems impassable, God is already preparing the way.

The Song of the Sea

Overcome with awe and gratitude after crossing the sea, the Jewish people burst into song.

"Then Moses and the children of Israel sang this song to God, and they spoke, saying, 'I will sing to God, for He has triumphed gloriously; horse and rider He has cast into the sea!'" (Exodus 15:1)

This was no ordinary song. It was a spontaneous, prophetic expression of faith, gratitude and joy—an eternal testimony to God's mastery over nature and history. This song, known as *Shirat HaYam* (The Song of the Sea), is recorded in the Bible (Exodus 15:1-19) and is recited daily in Jewish prayer. On the last day of Passover, we read this section as the Torah reading for the day, reliving the experience of that miraculous moment.

The song describes God's unparalleled might, His love for His people, and His promise to bring them to the land of Israel. It's a song of victory, but also of faith—the recognition that every step of redemption is guided by divine providence. The final verse resounds with a declaration that has echoed throughout Jewish history: "God will reign forever and ever." (Exodus 15:18)

Joy Finds Its Voice

The splitting of the sea marked the completion of Israel's freedom — that much we've established. But Rabbi Obadiah Seforno offers a different perspective on why this day became a permanent festival. It wasn't the miracle that made the day holy. It was the song.

"On the seventh day after the Exodus from Egypt the Israelites took time out to sing a song of thanksgiving to God for their final delivery from the pursuing Egyptians. Subsequently, in commemoration of that occasion, the Torah decreed that this day become an *atzeret*, a day devoted to contemplation of the great miracle on that first occasion."[5]

It was the nation's heartfelt expression of gratitude and joy that made this day special.

The Talmud teaches that song is the ultimate expression of joy.[6] The Splitting of the Sea wasn't just another miracle—it was the moment when the Jewish people finally felt free enough, relieved enough, and grateful enough to break into song. According to Seforno and others, this joy is the essence of the seventh day of Passover.

Think about it: they had witnessed plagues in Egypt. They had experienced the first Passover sacrifice. They had left their homes and

---

5. Seforno on Leviticus 23:36 On the seventh day after the Exodus from Egypt the Israelites took time out to sing a song of thanksgiving to God for their final delivery from the pursuing Egyptians. Subsequently, in commemoration of that occasion, the Torah decreed that this day become an □□□□, a day devoted to contemplation of the great miracle on that first occasion.

6. *Arachin* 11a

walked into the wilderness. But it was only at the sea, only when they were fully, irrevocably free, that their joy finally found its voice.

Miriam and the Women's Song

While Moses led the men in song, Miriam, Moses' sister and a prophetess in her own right, took up her timbrel and led the women in their own celebration:

"And Miriam the prophetess, the sister of Aaron, took the timbrel in her hand, and all the women followed her with timbrels and dances. And Miriam called out to them: 'Sing to God, for He has triumphed gloriously; horse and rider He has cast into the sea!'" (Exodus 15:20-21)

Miriam's leadership in song reflects the unique spiritual strength of women. While the men sang their praises, the women did so with music and dance, demonstrating deep and exuberant joy.

But here's what makes this even more remarkable: The sages explain that the righteous women of that generation had prepared their timbrels in Egypt, trusting with certainty that God would perform miracles for them.[7] Think about that. While still enslaved, while still oppressed, they packed musical instruments—not essentials for survival, but instruments of celebration. Their faith, expressed in both preparation and celebration, teaches that true belief isn't just about witnessing miracles but about living with the certainty that God is guiding us.

---

7. Rashi on Exodus 15:20

How We Observe This Day

The final day of Passover is a full festival day, similar to the first day. The prohibition against work is in place, just as on the Sabbath, with the exception of activities necessary for food preparation.

Special prayers are recited in the synagogue, including *Hallel* (Psalms of praise) and the Torah reading of The Song of the Sea. The *Yizkor* memorial prayer is also recited in remembrance of departed loved ones.

Two festive meals are held, one at night and one during the day, both beginning with *Kiddush* (the sanctification of the day over wine) and the blessing over two pieces of *matzah*. These meals serve not only as moments of physical enjoyment but also as opportunities to reflect on the themes of redemption and faith.

The Meal of the Messiah

As the final day of Passover draws to a close, some have the custom to hold one last meal — not to celebrate the past, but to anticipate the future. It is called *Seudat Mashiach*, the Meal of the Messiah, a tradition introduced by the Baal Shem Tov (c. 1698-1760), founder of Hasidic Judaism.

This meal highlights the deep connection between the Exodus from Egypt and the ultimate redemption to come. Just as the first day of Passover marks the beginning of our journey to freedom—when God redeemed the Israelites from Egypt through Moses, the first redeemer—the last day looks ahead to the completion of that journey, when God will bring the final redemption through the Messiah.

The prophet Jeremiah promises that this final redemption will be so overwhelming that it will eclipse the very Exodus we've spent the week celebrating:

"Assuredly, a time is coming—declares the Lord—when it shall no more be said, 'As the Lord lives, who brought the Israelites out of the land of Egypt,' but rather, 'As the Lord lives, who brought out and led the offspring of the House of Israel from the northland and from all the lands to which I have banished them.' And they shall dwell upon their own soil." (Jeremiah 23:7-8)

This is what we anticipate at the Meal of the Messiah. We've just relived the greatest redemption in our history—and we're declaring our faith that an even greater one is still to come, one that will complete what began in Egypt.

May we merit to see it soon.

An Eighth Day?

Passover, as the Torah commands it, is a seven-day holiday. Yet for Jews living outside the Land of Israel, the celebration extends to eight days due to an ancient rabbinic decree. This practice has a fascinating historical origin.

In Temple times, the Jewish calendar wasn't fixed by calculation but by direct observation. When witnesses spotted the new moon, they would report to the *Sanhedrin* (the central Jewish religious authority in Jerusalem), who would then officially declare the start of the new month. Since months could be either 29 or 30 days long, the precise date of any holiday depended on which length the previous month had been.

The *Sanhedrin* would send messengers to inform Jewish communities about when the month began, which was crucial for calculating the dates of the holidays correctly. For Jews living close to Jerusalem, this information arrived in time. For those in distant lands, it didn't. Uncertain whether the holiday fell on one day or the next, these communities observed both days, ensuring that one of them would certainly be correct.

When Rabbi Hillel II established a fixed mathematical calendar in the fourth century, the practical need for the extra day disappeared. Yet communities outside Israel have continued the practice to this day — honoring the custom of their ancestors and keeping alive, in a small but real way, the memory of what it means to live far from home.

What Happens When Passover Ends

As night falls and the holiday of Passover comes to a close, we transition back into the regular rhythm of life. This transition is marked by *Havdalah*, a special ceremony that distinguishes between the sacred time of the holiday and the ordinary days that follow.

Unlike the *Havdalah* of the Sabbath, which includes a candle and spices, the *Havdalah* at the conclusion of Passover is recited only over a cup of wine.

For those who sold their *chametz* before Passover, the rabbi now formally buys it back, making it permissible to consume once again. However, not a crumb passes our lips until after *Havdalah* is recited.

Some have the custom of reciting *Havdalah* over beer, a drink forbidden during the holiday because it contains grain, demonstrating that we abstained from *chametz* only because of God's command, not because we dislike it.

With Passover over, we carefully pack away our special dishes and utensils, storing them for the following year. The regular kitchenware, which had been set aside for the duration of the holiday, is once again brought out.

The Journey Continues

Though we celebrate complete physical redemption on this final day of Pesach, the journey is far from over.

The Splitting of the Sea freed the Israelites from Egyptian bondage, but true freedom isn't simply the absence of oppression; it's the opportunity to live with meaning and purpose.

The Israelites weren't freed merely to wander the desert. They were freed *for* something: to receive the Torah at Mount Sinai and enter into a covenant with God. From there, they would journey to the land of Israel, where they could fully live out their divine mission as a light to the nations.

This is why, even as Passover concludes, the counting of the *Omer* continues—a daily count of forty-nine days from the Exodus to the giving of the Torah on *Shavuot*. The counting itself teaches that liberation and revelation are inseparable. We measure our progress from physical freedom to spiritual purpose.

Passover may be over, but the journey continues—from Egypt to Sinai, from Sinai to the Promised Land.

A Final Word

You've now experienced Passover from the inside—not as a historical curiosity, but as a living tradition that has shaped how millions of people understand redemption, covenant, and their relationship with God.

This isn't just Jewish history. The Exodus is the foundation of biblical faith itself. The God who redeemed Israel from Egypt is the same God you worship. The covenant at Sinai is the covenant that gave the world Scripture. When you understand how the Jewish people have lived this story for three millennia, you read your Bible differently.

You've seen that redemption is never just about escape. It's about purpose. Freedom matters because of what it makes possible—receiving God's law, building a holy nation, becoming a light to the world.

May this understanding of Passover deepen your own faith and strengthen your connection to the God who redeems His people. The journey that began in Egypt continues.

Collected Insights

The Invisible Hand: Tracing Redemption's True Path

Rabbi Elie Mischel

When we imagine redemption, we picture thunderous miracles. Walls of water splitting. Plagues raining down. Dramatic, earth-shattering events that transform reality in an instant. But what if salvation arrives not with a roar, but with a whisper?

The question facing us today is: how does redemption actually unfold? Will the final redemption mirror the Exodus, with spectacular, supernatural interventions that defy all logic? Or might God's deliverance unfold in a way we least expect?

The prophet Isaiah provides the answer:

"The smallest shall become a clan; The least, a mighty nation. I God will speed it in due time." Isaiah 60:22

This verse reveals two potential paths of redemption. "*Achishena*" (I will speed it) represents redemption that comes suddenly, with open and spectacular miracles—like the Exodus from Egypt, where God intervened with tremendous, supernatural displays of power. Whole nations would be overthrown in an instant, the laws of nature suspended, divine intervention manifest for all to see.

But there's another path: "*b'itah*" (in due time). This is redemption that unfolds slowly, almost imperceptibly. It arrives through natural processes, without dramatic miracles. No splitting seas. No pillars of fire. Just the steady, patient work of transformation happening beneath the surface.

In Jewish tradition, the first day of Passover marks a powerful liturgical shift. Throughout the winter months, prayers include a request for rain—powerful, dramatic precipitation that drenches the earth. Rain is essential during Israel's winter growing season, and when it doesn't come, famine follows. But on Passover, as the rainy season ends, these prayers change. Now, the focus turns to dew—a subtle, gentle moisture that appears almost unnoticed. This shift is profoundly symbolic. Rain crashes from the sky in powerful torrents, reshaping the landscape in moments. Dew, by contrast, appears silently. Each morning, it settles softly across the ground, barely noticed yet transforming the earth. Just as dew nourishes the earth without fanfare, redemption can work quietly and consistently, changing everything without a sound.

This pattern appears throughout Jewish history. The biblical narrative suggests divine intervention changes over time. After the First Temple's destruction, miracles became less theatrical. Occasional extraordinary events—like the Six-Day War, where Israel's miraculous victory defied all military logic—remind us that God's hand remains active, even when less visible.

But the clearest example of dew-like redemption is the rebirth of Israel itself. The modern history of Israel reveals God working through nature and time. Over the last century, we've witnessed the extraordinary rebirth of a nation. Jews returned from Yemen, Ethiopia, Russia, and a hundred other lands. Pioneers drained swamps and planted forests. Hebrew—a language of prayer for two thousand years—became the language of mothers singing lullabies to their babies. Cities rose from sand. The desert bloomed. A scattered people became a thriving nation. The land that lay desolate for centuries has been brought back to life. Prophecies once considered impossible have been fulfilled before our eyes. And none of it happened in a single miraculous moment. It happened drop by drop, year by year, generation by generation.

The prayer for dew captures this spirit of quiet transformation: "Dew, precious dew, unto Your land forlorn, Pour out our blessing in Your exultation, To strengthen us with ample wine and corn, And give Your chosen city safe foundation in dew."

When the Jews returned from Babylonian exile, they found Jerusalem in ruins. The Temple lay destroyed. The city's walls were shattered stones, a testament to devastating defeat. Despair could have easily consumed them. Many likely hoped for a miraculous, instantaneous restoration—a divine intervention that would rebuild everything in a moment.

But Nehemiah understood redemption differently. He taught the people that salvation doesn't always arrive like rain—sudden and overwhelming. Sometimes redemption comes like dew, gradually and quietly. He showed them that if each person would rebuild just their small section of the wall, eventually the entire city would be restored. One stone at a time. One section at a time.

This was not a minor accomplishment. It was a revolutionary understanding of redemption. Instead of waiting for a miraculous, complete restoration, they would participate actively in their own salvation. Each person took responsibility for their own small piece of the larger mission.

This is not passive waiting. This is active hope. We recognize that redemption arrives through persistent, faithful work. Small actions.

Quiet dedication. The gentle accumulation of effort, like dew gathering on morning grass.

Redemption is not a single moment, but a process. It demands patience, vision, and persistent faith. We are called to be partners in this unfolding miracle—to see beyond the immediate, to trust in a larger plan.

Our role is to continue building, supporting, and believing. To water the seeds of hope, drop by drop, until the landscape of our world is transformed.

A Sacred Love Story

Rabbi Elie Mischel

Song of Songs, read on the holiday of Passover, is written as a love story between a woman and her beloved. It describes a romantic relationship, often using very sensual language. At first glance, it seems out of place among the other books of the Bible. The Bible is holy. The love between man and woman is earthly and mundane. The book's passionate language seems inappropriate for a religious text.

Indeed, some translations refuse to translate Song of Songs literally, opting instead to provide only an allegorical interpretation. Since the literal language is too physical, they offer readers the "deeper" meaning of King Solomon's words.

But this raises an obvious question: why write it as a love story at all?

The question becomes even stronger when you consider the words of the great Talmudic sage, Rabbi Akiva, who said: "The entire universe is unworthy of the day that the Song of Songs was given to Israel, for all the Writings are holy, but Song of Songs is the Holy of Holies."[8]

Does this love story really sound like the "Holy of Holies"? Was the whole world created for this?

We can answer these questions with another question, one asked by Rabbi Chanoch Henoch of Alexander, a student of the Hasidic Rabbi Menachem Mendel of Kotzk (1787-1859). The *seder* is a special meal

---

8. Mishna Yadayim 3:5

eaten on Passover night. During this meal, the Exodus from Egypt is discussed in question-and-answer format, beginning with four specific questions. Yet we don't start the *seder* immediately with these four questions. If the point of the *seder* is to discuss the Exodus and ask these questions, why do we do a few other things first?

To answer this question, imagine the following scenario. A couple has been dating for some time, and things have been going well. They are sitting in a romantic spot when the man takes a deep breath and says to the woman: "I love you—will you marry me?" Assuming she feels the same way, how should she respond at this moment? Should she dive into: "But how will we support ourselves?" or "What will our families think?" These aren't bad questions. They're important questions! But they don't belong in that moment, because it is a moment that transcends questions.

Passover, when God took our forefathers out of Egypt, was that kind of moment—the engagement of an entire people to God. The story of Passover goes beyond the intellect. It is a reliving of that moment of engagement, that moment every couple remembers for the rest of their lives. First and foremost, Passover is about those extraordinary, raw, and powerful moments that we, every last one of our people, shared with God.

We don't begin the *seder* with the four questions because not everything is open to question. It is only after we speak about the uniquely close and loving relationship that we as a people have with God that we can begin to ask questions. If we started with questions right away, we would miss something deep, something essential. Because a relationship of real love, love that runs deeper than the mind, doesn't begin with logical questions.

This is what King Solomon was describing in Song of Songs, and this is what makes the book so unusual and spectacular. Song of Songs is about the love between God and His people. It is about those moments that come before questions! Song of Songs is not about religion; it is about God Himself!

This is why Song of Songs is considered "Holy of Holies." Religion is holy. Observing the Sabbath is holy. The Temple is holy. But there is something that goes beyond holy, and that is our relationship with God Himself. This is also why Song of Songs is read on Passover—because it was on Passover that the love story between God and his people began.

Who is a Wealthy Man?

Dina Cohn

In the 1950s, a distinguished Russian rabbi named Aharon Leib Steinman moved to the Land of Israel. The Holy Land was not very developed at the time, and when he finally arrived, he moved into a tiny apartment with only the most basic furniture. Despite the meager accommodations, Rabbi Steinman never complained and was always grateful for what he had.

Over the years, the rabbi's brilliance and holiness gained worldwide recognition, attracting countless students to his house of study. In time, he became known as one of the most outstanding rabbis of his era.

Upon Rabbi Steinman's passing in 2017, his family observed the seven-day mourning period. Friends and admirers from far and wide converged on his home to offer condolences and pay tribute to his remarkable life. It was during this time that many people came to appreciate how simply Rabbi Steinman had lived. For over six decades, he had resided in the same modest apartment and slept on the same thin mattress he had been given upon arrival. His bedroom had doubled as his office—a testament to his humble lifestyle.

Rabbi Steinman understood something fundamental about wealth and contentment. This same truth appears in the last verses of Song of Songs.

In the final chapter of Song of Songs, the narrator has found peace in her relationship with her beloved. She has also found peace within herself. The once-confused young woman is finally exactly where she wants to be.

The last few verses of the book, however, seem puzzling. Verses 11-12 read:

"Solomon had a vineyard in Baal-hamon. He had to post guards in the vineyard: A man would give for its fruit a thousand pieces of silver. I have my very own vineyard: You may have the thousand, O Solomon, And the guards of the fruit, two hundred!" (Song of Songs 8:11-12)

What is the meaning of this parable of Solomon's vineyard? And how does it fit with the narrator's newfound confidence?

Biblical commentators explain that the narrator is expressing her contentment with what she already has. She had the opportunity to marry a king but pursued her beloved instead. She does not want any part of Solomon's vineyard or the wealth that comes with it. She has her own vineyard and declares that Solomon need not give any of his to her. She is happier with what she has now—what she wanted all along: her beloved. Having found contentment in her relationship, the narrator recognizes the futility of desiring what someone else has. Instead, she finds happiness in what she already possesses.

Ethics of the Fathers expresses this principle simply: "Ben Zoma says: Who is rich? He who rejoices in his lot."

Rabbi Steinman and the narrator of Song of Songs both understood this truth: happiness is not determined by material possessions or wealth. The true measure of wealth lies in finding contentment in what one already has—whether through family, work, or relationships with loved ones. This sense of fulfillment cannot be replaced by any amount of riches. True contentment comes from valuing what matters most, not from pursuing material gain.

As we read Song of Songs on the holiday of Passover, a time to ponder freedom, this message is worth keeping in mind. What type of contentment truly makes us free? True freedom comes not from material wealth or possessions, but from finding joy in our present circumstances.

The Path to Loving God

Yehoshua Rose

A brief read of Song of Songs can raise the eyebrows of even the most open-minded adherents to religion. "What is such an explicit and graphic piece of literature doing in my Bible?" Some of the more surprising quotes include:

"Scarcely had I passed them when I found the one I love. I held him fast, I would not let him go Till I brought him to my mother's house, To the chamber of her who conceived me" (Song of Songs 3:4).

"Your lips are like a crimson thread, Your mouth is lovely. Your brow behind your veil [Gleams] like a pomegranate split open" (Song of Songs 4:3).

Jewish tradition teaches that Song of Songs is an extended metaphor for the relationship between God and His chosen nation. But God is above all physicality. How, then, does Song of Songs provide an accurate representation of the relationship between Man and God?

To answer this question we must first ask another. The verses in Deuteronomy (6:4-9), known to Jewish people as the *Shema* prayer, are recited at least twice a day by all practicing Jews. The opening words to verse 6:5 read: "You shall love *Hashem* your God with all your heart and with all your soul and with all your might." It's hard enough to love family and friends, other humans of flesh and blood. How are we expected to achieve the sublime goal of loving an infinite being?

To answer both questions, we need to return to the first, for it is Song of Songs that provides the answer.

The ultimate expression of human love is the intimate bond of marriage between a man and a woman—the total integration of two bodies, two souls, into one unified entity. Yet the Torah does not describe this as God's initial plan.

The first chapter of Genesis describes God initially creating man and woman as one entity: "And *Hashem* created man in His image, in the image of *Hashem* He created him; male and female He created them" (Genesis 1:27). This unified creation was placed in the Garden of Eden, "to serve and guard it." This was Adam's way of serving God—achieving connection with God by upholding and preserving the garden. But just two verses later, there is a realization that to serve God, Adam needs another avenue to reach these spiritual heights.

God extracts a part of Adam and uses it to form Eve. Adam alone is now, by his very nature, incomplete. He is profoundly lacking. To become complete again, he must return to his "fitting helper" (Genesis 2:18).

The root used to express the union between man and woman is "*d,v,k*," which means to cling or to cleave (Genesis 2:24). Interestingly, we find the identical root used to describe man's connection to God:

"Hence a man leaves his father and mother and clings to his wife, so that they become one flesh." (Genesis 2:24)

"You must revere *Hashem* your God: only Him shall you worship, to Him shall you hold fast (cling), and by His name shall you swear." (Deuteronomy 10:20)

God's swift decision to create a helpmate for Man, and the identical use of the word "*davak*," indicate something profound. A person achieves the ultimate bond and love of God by first developing that connection with a human partner. Man's connection with his human partner is the prerequisite for connection with his infinite partner.

This gives us the framework underlying Song of Songs. King Solomon chose the metaphor of two lovers because that is the ultimate conduit for Man to develop a connection with the Almighty.

The great medieval sage Maimonides (1138–1204), in describing the proper way to love God, uses this exact structure:

"What is the proper [degree] of love? That a person should love God with a very great and exceeding love until his soul is bound up in the love of God. Thus, he will always be obsessed with this love as if he is lovesick. [A lovesick person's] thoughts are never diverted from the love of that woman. He is always obsessed with her; when he sits down, when he gets up, when he eats and drinks. With an even greater [love], the love for God should be [implanted] in the hearts of those who love Him and are obsessed with Him at all times as we are commanded [Deuteronomy 6:5: "Love God...] with all your heart and with all soul." This concept was implied by Solomon [Song of Songs 2:5] when he stated, as a metaphor: "I am lovesick." [Indeed,] the totality of the Song of Songs is a parable describing [this love]."[9]

The passionate love described by King Solomon is now understood: the pursuit of deep human love gives us the means and ability to achieve love with the Divine.

---

9. Laws of Repentance 10:3

Chasing the King

Dina Cohn

A man once recounted the following story on an Israeli radio station. He had been brought to England on the *Kindertransport*, a rescue mission that saved Jewish children from Nazi Germany, and grew up in an orphanage. One day, a thrilling announcement was made—King George VI was coming to visit their orphanage!

The excited children were instructed to put on their best clothes for the occasion. They lined up outside, eagerly waiting for the king's arrival. But their excitement turned to disappointment when they realized they would only see the king drive by—not meet him face to face. Disappointment filled their hearts as they stood there, watching the king's car approach.

But then something unexpected happened. One of the boys broke ranks and started chasing after the car. He ran as fast as he could, knocking against the car until it finally stopped. The door opened, and the boy found himself face to face with the king!

King George VI asked the boy what was wrong, and the boy explained that he had been hoping to meet the king to express his gratitude for bringing him to safety in England. "But you see," he continued, "I'm terribly lonely. My parents are still over there." The king listened patiently, asking for the boy's name and where he was from. He thanked the boy for his kind words and bid him farewell.

Just a few weeks later, the headmaster of the orphanage called the boy into his office. The boy was nervous, not knowing what he could have possibly done wrong. To his amazement, the headmaster revealed that the king had been deeply moved by their encounter. He opened a side door, and there stood the boy's parents.

The man who recounted this story ended with regret. He had spent the last 60 years asking himself why he had not done the same and chased after the king.

We feel for the man who spent his life wondering why he hadn't taken the chance to approach the king as that brave little boy did. Maybe his story could have had a different ending. We all have a chance to chase after the King. Do we take the opportunity when it is presented, or do we live our lives regretting the missed opportunities?

One of the most powerful portions of Song of Songs is found in Chapter 5. Song of Songs was written by King Solomon about the love between a man and a woman, and is an allegory for the love between God and the Children of Israel. In chapter 5, the narrator is found in her bed, her heart alive with emotion, when she hears her beloved knocking at the door. He pleads that she let him in—at long last, her beloved has come to her! But she hesitates:

"I had taken off my robe— Was I to don it again? I had bathed my feet— Was I to soil them again?" (Song of Songs 5:3)

After a moment, she returns to her senses and rushes to open the door, but it is too late. Her beloved is gone. She calls out to her beloved, but there is no answer. Heartbroken, she runs out into the night, searching desperately for her lover.

How are we to understand this section? Why does the narrator hesitate? Her beloved was right at her door—was she too lazy to get up and let him in?

Mrs. Michal Horowitz, a contemporary Bible scholar, references the medieval commentator Rashi to help us understand these verses. According to Rashi, the entire book of Song of Songs is a metaphor for the Jewish people in Exile. After being "betrothed" to God on Mount Sinai, the Jewish people "cheated" on Him with the Golden Calf and the Sin of the Spies, among other sins. God eventually sent the Jewish people into exile for their sins, just as a husband would send away a cheating wife. However, God loves the Jewish people so much that He continues to check in on them, even in their exile.

This is the deeper meaning of Song of Songs. The lover who waits behind the walls, watching for his beloved through the window and waiting for her to seek him out once again, is a metaphor for God who watches over His people in the Exile and longs for their return.

The narrator, a metaphor for the Children of Israel, is too complacent in her Exile. She's intoxicated by the wine, myrrh, and honey (verse 1), enjoying herself too much. By the time her lover gets to her door, she has had a full day, gotten ready for bed, and is about to sleep. She hears her lover knocking but thinks to herself, 'How can I put on my robe again? I've already settled in for the night.'

This hesitation represents something deeper: she feels so entrenched in her life of exile that returning seems impossible. In the next verse, the lover peeks through the latch one last time to see if his beloved is still there. This simple action creates a shift in the narrator's perspective. She realizes she has made a mistake and rushes out of bed to open the door before it is too late. But her beloved is gone.

The man who was saved on the *Kindertransport* never got a second chance to meet the king, but the narrator of Song of Songs does. Even before this chapter, she has had many chances—her beloved is always waiting for her to come back. The bond between God and His children is never broken, and He is always ready and willing to take us back.

As children of God, we always have the opportunity to come back to Him. He is always waiting for us to return and repent. It is up to us whether we seize the opportunities that come our way or let them pass us by. Though we may sometimes feel too entrenched in our current situation, like the narrator of Song of Songs, it is never too late to make a change. We can choose to chase after the King because He's waiting. Because the door is still open. Because, unlike the man from the orphanage, we haven't missed our chance. God stands at the door and knocks, and the only question is: will we get up and answer?

God's Perpetual Love

Yehoshua Rose

Song of Songs is unique in the Bible. Even books such as Psalms, Jeremiah, and Isaiah, which contain beautiful poetic writings, are distinctly different from Song of Songs.

It is a deep, emotive love song that, at face value, seems very out of place among the writings of Scripture. But despite its unique, almost transgressive nature, the great sage Rabbi Akiva said in the *Mishna*: "All [Biblical] writings are holy, but Song of Songs is the holiest of the holies."[10] There is more to this Biblical book than meets the eye.

The great Jewish Biblical commentators understood that although couched in the metaphor of a love song, Song of Songs expresses a deeper truth. It is a conversation between God and His chosen people. Throughout the eight chapters of the book, God is called "*dodi*," "my beloved," while "*rayati*," "my darling"—the fair maiden—represents God's people.

The *Targum*, the Aramaic translation and commentary of Song of Songs, notes that there were ten other divinely inspired songs composed throughout history. These range from Adam's praise of God at the onset of the first Sabbath, to songs of gratitude following military victories, to the ultimate composition to be sung upon the arrival of

10. Mishna Yadayim 3:5

the final redemption.[11] Yet, as Rabbi Shimshon Pinkus (1944–2001) notes, Song of Songs is uniquely different.

The ten songs noted by the *Targum* are expressions of success in some domain of life: Hannah's song of joy after her prayers to God were answered and she was granted a child; the song sung by the Jewish people after successfully crossing the Reed Sea; the final song after the arrival of the redemption. Song of Songs is fundamentally different. Unlike the other songs, it is not a depiction of triumph and achievement but the complicated expression of a relationship between God and His people. As with any loving relationship, its story cannot be reduced to golden moments of success. It is a journey down the road of struggle, error, and strain. But what binds the travelers together is their unbreakable desire to continue along the trail together.

The opening words of Dickens's *A Tale of Two Cities* capture the underlying message and complexity of Song of Songs:

"It was the best of times, it was the worst of times, it was the age of wisdom, it was the age of foolishness... it was the season of Light, it was the season of Darkness, it was the spring of hope, it was the winter of despair, we had everything before us, we had nothing before us, we were all going direct to Heaven, we were all going direct the other way..."

Song of Songs is a voyage through Biblical history. It is the twists and turns of two lovers who are ultimately bonded together for eternity. From the peaks of the Exodus to the lows of the Sin of the Golden Calf; from the grandeur of the Temple to its ultimate destruction.

11. Targum, Shir HaShirim 1:1

Song of Songs is a roller coaster through a tense but deep relationship. There are ups, and there are downs. But ultimately God declares to His people (8:7), "Vast floods cannot quench love, Nor rivers drown it. If a man offered all his wealth for love, He would be laughed to scorn."

The great medieval commentator Rashi understands that this verse is God communicating the following message: "Vast floods"—the nations of the world—"cannot quench [the] love"—the love that God has for His people. "Nor rivers"—even the actions of kings and princes—"[cannot] drown it." Even using strength, fear, intimidation, and seduction, God's love will endure.

During the good times, the Jewish People adhere to God's word. They follow His commandments, learn His Torah, and heed His advice. But throughout the Bible, this always seems to come to an end all too soon. Quickly, the nation descends into sinful behavior. Gone are the days of devotion to the Almighty, and in its place, wayward and defiant behavior emerges. The maiden has betrayed the one who loves her.

Song of Songs expresses this perpetual paradox in verse 1:5:

"I am black but comely, O daughters of Jerusalem! Like the tents of Kedar, like the curtains of Solomon."

Rabbi Baruch ha-Levi Epstein (1860–1941), in his work *Torah Temimah*, details the stark contrasts expressed within this single sentence. Among the over ten different Biblical events hinted at in this verse, Rabbi Epstein suggests:

"Dark" is a reference to the disobedience toward God while in the land of Egypt; "Comely" refers to ultimate adherence to His commandments upon fulfilling the Paschal lamb sacrifice. Alternatively, "Dark" hints at the actions on the shores of the Reed Sea when God was criticized: "Was it for want of graves in Egypt that you brought us to die in the wilderness? What have you done to us, taking us out of Egypt?" "Comely" is a hint to the spontaneous outburst of joy and gratitude when the sea split and the nation was saved. "Dark" is an indication of the slander the spies expressed after journeying around the land of Israel; "Comely" is a reference to the righteous actions of Joshua and Caleb when they defended the beauty and integrity of the land.

Rabbi Epstein lists several other self-contradictory Biblical events, but the examples above suffice to illustrate the idea. The Jewish people's relationship with God is anything but smooth sailing.

Yet despite the rocky road, the prophet Isaiah gives us reassurance that, notwithstanding Israel's errant ways and consistent shortcomings, God's love remains steadfast and the unbreakable bond He has with His nation endures.

"For the mountains may move and the hills be shaken, But my loyalty shall never move from you, Nor My covenant of friendship be shaken —said God, who takes you back in love." (Isaiah 54:10)

This is why Song of Songs is read on Passover. The holiday commemorates not just physical redemption but the beginning of an eternal relationship—a bond forged in Egypt that has weathered every trial since. No matter how many times the relationship has been strained, God's love remains constant. The covenant endures. And the beloved continues to call out, waiting for his people to return.

Who Needs the End of Passover?

Rabbi Elie Mischel

Growing up, I waited all year long for the first night of Passover, when we, like Jewish families all over the world, would celebrate the magical *seder* night. Since my parents did all the cooking and hard work to prepare for the *seder*, the first night, for me, was pure joy (except for the 20 minutes of heartburn I'd suffer after drinking too much sweet wine!).

There was only one problem: the first night of Passover was so great, the rest of the holiday felt like a letdown! I could never understand why God wanted us to celebrate for seven days, and why the last day of Passover is considered as holy as the first.

Only as I grew older did I discover the secret holiness of the last day of Passover.

During the first days of Passover, we re-experience the Exodus, God's awesome redemption of the people of Israel from the slavery of Egypt. It was the first time in history that God redeemed His people.

But the Kabbalists explain that on the last days of Passover, our hearts and our minds turn from the first redemption to the final redemption of Israel.

On the last days of Passover, Jews traditionally read two passages from the prophets that reflect our yearning for the final redemption.

First, we read from David's final song of praise to God, in which David gives thanks to God for redeeming him from all of his enemies:

"David addressed the words of this song to the Lord, after the Lord had saved him from the hands of all his enemies and from the hands of Saul... All praise! I called on the Lord and was delivered from my enemies." (II Samuel 22:1,4)

David, God's anointed one, is the ancestor of the Messiah. His song of thanks to God at the end of his life, when he was finally safe and secure from all of his enemies, is meant to express our own yearning for the final redemption, when the people of Israel will finally be saved from all their enemies. By reading this passage at the end of Passover, we turn our attention from the original redemption from Egypt to the longed-for final redemption!

The second passage that we read at the end of Passover is taken from Isaiah, where the prophet beautifully describes the end of days when David's heir will redeem his people:

"But a shoot shall grow out of the stump of Jesse, A twig shall sprout from his stock. The spirit of God shall alight upon him: A spirit of wisdom and insight, A spirit of counsel and valor, A spirit of devotion and reverence for God. He shall sense the truth by his reverence for God: He shall not judge by what his eyes behold, Nor decide by what his ears perceive. Thus he shall judge the poor with equity and decide with justice for the lowly of the land. He shall strike down a land with the rod of his mouth and slay the wicked with the breath of his lips." (Isaiah 11:1-4)

From the passages we read at the end of the holiday, it is clear that the end of Passover is no mere afterthought. To the contrary! It is the most awesome moment of the entire year, when we bring to the surface and express, through song and prayer, thousands of years of pain and longing for redemption!

The sages teach that "in the Hebrew month of *Nisan* we were [originally] redeemed [through the Exodus from Egypt], and in the Hebrew month of *Nisan* we will once again be redeemed in the future."[12] The holiday of Passover is not only a time to remember and celebrate our original redemption, when God brought the people of Israel out of Egypt and made them His chosen nation. The holiday of Passover is also the time when God will one day bring the final redemption!

For this reason, during the final hours of Passover, Jews all over the world celebrate the "Meal of the Messiah." As the sun sets and the final day of Passover draws to a close, we once again sing passages of faith from the *Haggadah*. Only this time, we sing not to remember the past, but to express our longing for the future, when God will remove all of our pain and bring joy and gladness to the entire world.

May we soon see that day!

---

12. Babylonian Talmud, Rosh Hashanah 11a

Stop Praying and Jump

Shira Schechter

Seven days after leaving Egypt, three million Israelites stood trapped between the sea and Pharaoh's approaching army. God had commanded them to move forward, but the sea hadn't split. They couldn't go back because the Pharaoh's army was in hot pursuit. There was no way out, and the people panicked.

"As Pharaoh drew near, the Israelites caught sight of the Egyptians advancing upon them. Greatly frightened, the Israelites cried out to Hashem. And they said to Moshe, "Was it for want of graves in Egypt that you brought us to die in the wilderness? What have you done to us, taking us out of Egypt?" Exodus 14:10-11

Then Nahshon son of Amminadab, a prince of Judah, walked into the water.

Nahshon was a fifth-generation descendant of Judah, son of Jacob. From this line would come King David and eventually the Messiah. Leadership was in Nahshon's blood.

We first encounter him in a family context: "Aaron took for a wife Elisheva, daughter of Amminadab, sister of Nahshon" (Exodus 6:23). Through his sister's marriage to Aaron, Nahshon became brother-in-law to Israel's first High Priest. He stood at the intersection of tribal leadership and spiritual authority—but his defining moment came not through position or pedigree, but through action.

The sages fill in the details that the Bible itself leaves out. While everyone else hesitated, not wanting to jump into the sea, Nahshon took action.[13]

He didn't wait for the miracle. He didn't demand proof that God would save him. He simply understood that God had commanded forward movement, and forward movement required someone to move forward. So he did.

The water reached his ankles. Nothing happened. He continued. Water to his knees. Still no miracle. Deeper still—waist, chest, neck. The sea hadn't budged. At the very last moment, as water reached his nostrils and death seemed certain, the sea split.

The sages add a striking detail. While Nahshon was drowning, Moses was praying. God said to him, "My beloved ones are drowning in the stormy seas, and you are standing and praying?"

Moses protested: "Master of the world, what am I to do?"

God's answer: "You lift your staff and spread your hand over the seas, which will split, and Israel will come into the sea upon dry land" (Exodus 14:16)

Prayer has its place. But sometimes God is waiting for action.

Nahshon's name has become synonymous with the courage to obey God's command even when obedience seems impossible. King David, inspired by this ancestor, wrote in Psalms: "I have sunk in muddy depths, and there is no place to stand; I have come into the deep water,

---

13. Mekhilta de-Rabbi Ishmael, Beshalach, Section 6

and the current has swept me away... Let the floodwaters not sweep me away; let the deep not swallow me; let the mouth of the Pit not close over me" (Psalms 69:3, 16).

David understood: Faith isn't passive. Faith means stepping into the flood.

Rabbi Menachem Mendel Schneerson captured the lesson: "One fellow named Nahshon jumped into the sea, and caused the great miracle of the Splitting of the Sea. Technically, he was under no obligation to do so. But he knew that God wanted Israel to move onward toward Sinai. So he did what he needed to do. There was a sea in his way. So he jumped into the sea and plowed on toward his goal."

The Rebbe continued: "The lesson for all of us is that we must stay focused on our life's mission, disregarding all obstacles."[14]

We face the Red Sea every time we must choose between comfort and calling, between the familiar and the necessary, between the safety of Egypt and the risk of freedom. Egypt wasn't just geography—it was the mindset that says "stay put, don't risk, wait for someone else." The sea wasn't just water—it was every obstacle that seems too big, every challenge that appears insurmountable, every moment when the easier choice is to do nothing.

Nahshon teaches that sometimes the miracle doesn't come before the commitment. It comes after. God was ready to split the sea, but He was waiting for someone to trust Him enough to take the first step.

---

14. Rabbi Menachem Mendel Schneerson, https://www.chabad.org/library/article_cdo/aid/2199147/jewish/Nachshon-ben-Aminadav-The-Man-Who-Jumped-Into-the-Sea.htm

How many opportunities have we missed because we waited for conditions to be perfect? How many times has God been ready to act, waiting only for us to move forward in obedience to His will?

Nahshon wasn't superhuman. He was a man who simply refused to let fear prevent him from obeying God's command. He looked at the same sea everyone else saw. He heard the same chariots approaching. But he made a different choice.

God was going to save Israel. He had promised it. He had commanded them forward. The miracle was His doing. But Nahshon chose to respond in faith rather than fear. He chose obedience over hesitation. And when one man moved forward, three million followed.

The question isn't whether we'll face our own Red Seas. We will. The question is whether we'll respond to God's command with faith or with fear—whether we'll step forward in obedience or wait for someone else to go first.

The sea is before us. The choice is ours.

What are We Waiting for?

Rabbi Elie Mischel

Redemption!

Everyone who truly believes in the Bible yearns for the day when this world will be redeemed. But what, really, are we yearning for?

On the final day of Passover outside of Israel, we read Isaiah's extraordinary words:

"The wolf shall dwell with the lamb, The leopard lie down with the kid; The calf, the beast of laws of prey, and the fatling together, With a little boy to herd them." Isaiah 11:6

When we read these words, we imagine redemption as a time when the very laws of nature will change – when wolves and lambs will stroll down the boardwalk together, arm in arm, and enjoy a lovely dinner together at the beach!

But is this world of fantasy what we are waiting for?

The sages tell a fascinating story:

"Rabbi Joseph, the son of Rabbi Joshua, became ill and fell into a trance. When he recovered, his father asked him, 'What did you see?' Rabbi Joseph said: 'I saw an upside-down world, where those who are great here are low there, and those who are low here are great there.'

'My son,' said Rabbi Joshua, 'you [did not see an upside-down world. You] saw a clear world.'"[15]

We believe that we are living in a "normal" world, for this is the only world we know. And we believe that at the end of days, the Messiah will bring all of us to another world, a holy world, altogether different from the world we know.

But the truth is quite different. It is our world, the world we are living in today, that is not normal! Our world, filled with falsehood and deceit, is upside down!

In our world, evil people are successful, while good people too often suffer. We live in a world that venerates athletes more than teachers, a world obsessed with satisfying temptation and desire, a world in which the things that matter most are ignored!

Because we are so used to living in this topsy-turvy world, we hardly notice how upside down it truly is. We're like people who lived through the era of slavery and assumed it was natural—they couldn't imagine a world without it.

What will redemption be like? What kind of world are we waiting for?

We are waiting for a clear and normal world, where the strong will no longer oppress the weak, and peace among nations will no longer be a dream.

This is the world that Isaiah describes! When he says "The wolf shall dwell with the lamb," he is not describing a world of fantasy in which

---

15. Babylonian Talmud, Pesachim 50a

the laws of nature are suspended. He is describing a world like ours – except that it will no longer be upside down!

As the great Maimonides writes:

"Do not presume that in the Messianic age any facet of the world's nature will change or there will be innovations in the work of creation. Rather, the world will continue according to its pattern. Although Isaiah states: 'The wolf will dwell with the lamb, the leopard will lie down with the young goat,' these words are a metaphor and a parable. The prophecy means that Israel will dwell securely together with those evil nations who are likened to a wolf and a leopard... They will all return to the true faith and no longer steal or destroy."[16]

As we conclude the holiday of Passover, the holiday of redemption, let us strengthen our belief in redemption. And let us pray for the day when our world will once again be "normal"!

---

16. Laws of Kings and Wars 12:1

Conclusion: Why Passover Is Your Story Too

You have spent this book learning how Jews observe Passover — the preparation, the *Seder*, the songs, the rituals, the foods, the texts. You have, in a sense, sat at a Jewish table. Before we part ways, I want to speak directly to you as a Christian reader and explain why none of this is merely interesting background — why, in fact, this may be the most important thing you ever learn about your own faith.

The Bible Is a Jewish Book

Let us begin with something simple that is easy to forget. The Bible you hold, the scripture you have read your entire life, the sacred text on which your entire faith rests — it is a Jewish book. Not metaphorically, not in some technical historical sense, but actually and completely a Jewish book, written by Jews, about Jews, addressed to Jews, and lived by Jews for thousands of years. The Hebrew Bible is not just a prologue or an introduction to the New Testament. It is God's eternal word.

This means that without understanding how Jews actually read and live the Bible — not as an abstraction but as a practice, a culture, a pulse — Christians will forever read their own scripture from the outside. Passover is the place to begin, because Passover is the heartbeat of the entire Hebrew Bible. Every covenant, every prophet, every psalm of redemption references and builds off of the Exodus.

The God of the Bible does not introduce Himself to the world primarily as Creator. He introduces Himself as the One who took His people out of Egypt, out of the house of slavery. That is the foundational divine act. That is the God of your Bible.

The Language Your Scripture Speaks

The New Testament is saturated with references to Passover. Redemption, sacrifice, the lamb, the blood, the unleavened bread, the cup of blessing, the night of vigil, the firstborn, the crossing of water into freedom — these are not generic religious metaphors. They are specific, precise, loaded references that carry their full meaning only against the backdrop of a Jewish Passover. Without that backdrop, you are reading in translation in the deepest possible sense.

The Last Supper took place in a Jewish Passover context, at a *Seder* table, with Jewish disciples, using the specific ritual structure that Jews have followed for millennia. Understanding what a *Seder* actually is illuminates what was happening in that room.

Redemption Is Not Only Spiritual

There is a tendency in much of Western Christianity to spiritualize and individualize redemption — to locate it entirely in the soul, in the afterlife, in the personal. Passover pushes back, powerfully. The redemption God performed at the Exodus was national, physical, historical, and collective. An entire people was freed from slavery. A nation was born. The liberation was real — mud on their feet, unleavened bread baked in haste, the sea split before them.

This matters for how you read the Bible. God cares about flesh and blood, about history, about peoples and nations. The God of Passover acts in the world.

The Chosenness of Israel and the Crisis of Our Moment

And this brings us to something that cannot be avoided in the world we are living in today.

Israel is under attack — militarily, diplomatically, and increasingly in the arena of Christian thought. There are voices in the Christian world today, prominent voices with large audiences, who have begun to deny or dismiss the chosenness of Israel. They question whether God's covenant with the Jewish people is real, whether Israel's presence in its land is legitimate, whether the biblical story of a chosen nation still means anything at all.

This is not a political disagreement. This is heresy. It is a direct denial of the Bible.

Passover is the celebration of that chosenness. "You have chosen us from all the nations." God looked down at a world of peoples and chose one — not because of their power or their numbers, for they were slaves with nothing — but because of His covenant with Abraham, Isaac, and Jacob, and because He intended, through this people, to bring His word and His purpose to the world. The Exodus is the foundational declaration that this people belongs to God and that God belongs to this people.

A Christian who denies the chosenness of the Jewish people is not taking a bold or independent theological stance. They are sawing off the branch on which their entire faith rests. You cannot affirm the God of the Bible and reject His covenant with Israel. You cannot revere the prophets and dismiss the people through whom every word of prophecy was given. You cannot claim to love the scripture and deny the nation that carried it through history at unimaginable cost.

Christians who stand with Israel today — and there are millions of them, and they are the greatest friends the Jewish people have — must understand *what* they are standing with. Not just a modern state, not just a political ally, but the living continuation of a covenant that goes back to Egypt, to the burning bush, to a night when God passed over the houses of His people and made them His own forever.

True Partnership Requires True Knowledge

Real friendship between Jews and Christians cannot be built on sentiment alone. If you want to stand with the Jewish people — genuinely, intelligently, faithfully — you must understand who we are. And no single window into who we are is as revealing as Passover. The foods we eat and why we eat them. The questions our children ask. The words we say at the table year after year: *This year we are slaves; next year may we be free. This year we are here; next year may we be in Jerusalem.*

You cannot love a people whose story you do not know.

I hope this book has given you that story. Not filtered through another tradition's interpretive lens, but as Jews actually live it — ancient and immediate, sorrowful and joyful, rooted in the past and stretching urgently toward the future.

Next year in Jerusalem!

www.ingramcontent.com/pod-product-compliance
Ingram Content Group UK Ltd.
Pitfield, Milton Keynes, MK11 3LW, UK
UKHW041629190726
13854UKWH00006B/2385

9 798988 440314